true discipleship

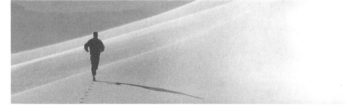

true discipleship

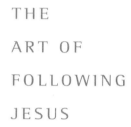

THE
ART OF
FOLLOWING
JESUS

JOHN KOESSLER

MOODY PUBLISHERS
CHICAGO

© 2003 by
JOHN KOESSLER

All Scripture quotations, unless otherwise indicated, are taken from the *Holy Bible, New International Version*®. NIV®. Copyright © 1973, 1978, 1984 by International Bible Society. Used by permission of Zondervan Publishing House. All rights reserved.

Scripture quotations marked NASB are taken from the *New American Standard Bible*®, © Copyright The Lockman Foundation 1960, 1962, 1963, 1968, 1971, 1972, 1973, 1975, 1977, 1995. Used by permission.

Scripture quotations marked KJV are taken from the King James Version.

Library of Congress Cataloging-in-Publication Data

Koessler, John, 1953-
    True discipleship : the art of following Jesus / John Koessler
        p. cm.
    Includes bibliographical references.
    ISBN 0-8024-1642-X
    1. Christian life. I. Title.

BV4501.3 .K64 2003
248.4—dc21

                                                                              2002151841

3 5 7 9 10 8 6 4 2

Printed in the United States of America

to Bob Johnson, John Natelborg, and Ron Seck

I am deeply grateful for all you have done
to help me understand what it means
to be a follower of Jesus Christ.

CONTENTS

ACKNOWLEDGMENTS

I am indebted to several people for the completion of this project. I am grateful to Jim Bell for encouraging me to write a book on discipleship after reading an article of mine on the subject in *Moody* magazine. I am also especially appreciative of the excellent editorial work of Jim Vincent and his keen eye for the heart of the matter in clarifying content and making needed cuts. My thanks also to Greg Thornton, publisher of Moody Publishers, for his support and enthusiasm for this project.

As always, my wife Jane's comments and encouragement helped shape my thinking and spurred me on when the process became tedious.

Last, but most importantly, I am grateful to God for extending His grace to me and for calling me to be a follower of His Son, Jesus Christ.

THE MARKS
OF DISCIPLESHIP

CHARACTERISTICS OF
A FOLLOWER OF CHRIST

After I graduated from college, I worked a few years for one of the major automobile companies. Some of that time was spent on the loading dock in a shipping and receiving department. During the summers, the heat inside the trucks that I helped to load could be suffocating. That could make the guys' tempers a little short.

One especially hot afternoon, as I was helping one of the drivers arrange his load, he grinned at me and said, "You're a religious man, aren't you?"

I was surprised by his question. This was the first time we had met, and our conversation in the few minutes we had been together hadn't progressed beyond the usual superficial observations about the weather.

"As a matter of fact, I am," I replied. "Why do you ask?"

"Oh, I noticed that you don't talk like the other fellas who help me," he answered. "Most of them would be cussing by now because of the heat. You haven't said one swear word."

I was pleased that he had seen something in my behavior that seemed to him to reflect genuine Christianity. Yet I was sobered by the reminder that others I worked with on a daily basis would also be looking for proof of the reality of my commitment to Christ. How consistent was I under the close scrutiny of those who knew me best? Did I have the marks of a genuine Christian?

When sharing my faith, I had often heard people respond by saying, "I used to know someone who believed like you do . . . " They would usually go on to describe some major character flaw reflected in that person's life. It was clear that my listeners felt such a shortcoming invalidated the other person's claim to the title of "Christian."

SOMETHING THAT SETS US APART

I would explain that Christians aren't sinless, only forgiven. But such reasoning hardly seemed convincing to them. If anything, my argument usually brought to mind other inconsistencies among those they knew who claimed to belong to Christ. The general assumption seemed to be that, although Christians aren't perfect, they should be different. There should be something that sets them apart as disciples. The Scriptures agree.

Horatius Bonar, the Scottish pastor and hymn writer of the nineteenth century, made this observation about the nature of the Christian life: "It is to new life that God is calling us; not to some new steps in life, some new habits or motives or prospects, but to *a new life*."[1]

Discipleship is not primarily a matter of what we do. It is an outgrowth of what we are. Yet if this is true, it is reasonable for others to expect to see proof of the reality of our commitment to Christ reflected in the way that we live. Jesus' observation regarding false prophets is also true of disciples. They are recognizable by the fruit they produce: "By their fruit you will recognize them. Do people pick grapes from thornbushes, or figs from thistles? Likewise every good tree bears good fruit, but a bad tree bears bad fruit" (Matthew 7:16–17).

So what are the marks of a disciple? Jesus Himself identified several important characteristics.

THE MARK OF BAPTISM

The first mark of a disciple is baptism. It is one of the first acts that identifies us as followers of Jesus Christ and initiates us into a life of obedience. When Jesus commissioned the church to go and make disciples of all nations, He identified baptism as the first of the two central tasks of disciple making (Matthew 28:19). After Christ's ascension, baptism continued to have a prominent place in apostolic preaching and practice. On the Day of Pentecost, the apostle Peter commanded those who believed to "repent and be baptized . . . in the name of Jesus Christ for the forgiveness of your sins. And you will receive the gift of the Holy Spirit" (Acts 2:38).

Although Christians differ over how baptism should take place (it has been done by sprinkling, pouring, and immersion), all agree that baptism is the initiatory rite of the Christian faith. John Calvin called it "the sign of the initiation by which we are received into the society of the church."[2]

It is a rite that has both individual and corporate significance. On the one hand, baptism symbolizes to observers and the individual alike the person's union with Christ in death and resurrection (Romans 6:3–4). At the same time, it signifies that the believer has also been joined to the larger fellowship of the church: "For we were all baptized by one Spirit into one body—whether Jews or Greeks, slave or free—and we were all given the one Spirit to drink" (1 Corinthians 12:13).

Baptism by water also symbolizes the believer's entrance into the sphere of the Holy Spirit.[3] The metaphor of drinking in 1 Corinthians 12:13 points to the Holy Spirit's ministry at our innermost level. The Holy Spirit is said to "live" in every believer and His controlling presence is more powerful than the presence of the sinful nature (Romans 8:9). But the benefit we receive from His ministry is not merely an individual one. Those who are individually joined to Christ by their union with the Spirit are also joined to one another. Water baptism signifies my entrance into the community of the Spirit.

Similarly, the symbolism of baptism serves as a public statement of the believer's personal commitment to Christ and conveys a promise from God to the believer. Baptism, according to John Calvin, is a public confession before men. "Indeed," he explained, "it is the mark by which we publicly profess that we wish to be reckoned God's people, by which we testify that we agree in worshipping the same God, in one religion with all Christians; by which finally we openly affirm our faith."[4] The apostle Peter used the legal language of contractual agreements to refer to baptism when he called it "the pledge of a good conscience toward God" in 1 Peter 3:21. The Greek term that is translated "pledge" literally meant "answer" and referred to a legal procedure in which questions were asked and commitments made on the part of those who entered into a contractual arrangement with one another. Baptism is a pledge of commitment made to God that springs from the cleansing that has come through faith in Christ.

On God's part, however, baptism contains an implied promise of forgiveness. New Testament preaching linked baptism to the promise of cleansing from sin (Acts 2:38; 22:16; cf. Mark 1:4; Luke 3:3). The connection between these two, however, is not an automatic one. The Bible does not teach that the rite of baptism in and of itself conveys the forgiveness of sin. Although Peter wrote that baptism "now saves you," he clarified that it is actually the resurrection of Christ that does the saving and not the water of baptism (1 Peter 3:21). When some in the Corinthian church began to boast about who had baptized them and divide into factions in the name of their favorite apostle, Paul wrote that he was glad that he had baptized so few. "For Christ did not send me to baptize," he declared, "but to preach the gospel" (1 Corinthians 1:17). Such a statement makes no sense if baptism is the means of obtaining forgiveness through Christ.

Because it symbolizes the believer's union with Christ through the Holy Spirit, baptism also contains an implicit promise of transformation. Baptism's picture of burial and resurrection points to a radical change in the believer's nature: "We were therefore buried with him through baptism into death in order that, just as Christ was raised from the dead through the glory of the Father, we too may live a new life" (Romans 6:4). Those who are in Christ are alive in a way that was not true prior to Christ.

The apostle Paul linked baptism with the Old Testament rite of circumcision and said that those who have been baptized have "put off" the old nature (Colossians 2:11–12). New Testament scholar C. E. B. Cranfield commented, "Paul expresses in the most decisive and emphatic way the truth of our having died with Christ; for burial is the seal set to the fact of death—it is when a man's relatives and friends leave his body in a grave and return home without him that the fact that he no longer shares their life is exposed with inescapable conclusiveness."[5]

All who enter into a relationship with Christ die to the old self. Positively, they have been "clothed" with Christ (Galatians 3:27).

God's promise in baptism is the promise of forgiveness and a new life. My commitment in baptism is the pledge to live in accordance with the change that Christ has brought about in me by His death and resurrection.

THE MARK OF OBEDIENCE

True discipleship is also marked by obedience. The second major component of Jesus' directive in the Great Commission was to teach disciples "to obey everything I have commanded you" (Matthew 28:20). Obedience is not optional for the Christian. As Jesus' popularity increased, He warned followers that obedience would be the true test of their discipleship. According to John 8:31–32, "To the Jews who had believed him, Jesus said, 'If you hold to my teaching, you are really my disciples. Then you will know the truth, and the truth will set you free.'"

Passages like this can make us uncomfortable because they seem to imply that our status as disciples is earned. There is a condition here, but its force is one of evidence rather than of cause. Jesus did not say that we become disciples by holding to His teaching. The obedience spoken of here proves that those who obey were truly His disciples in the first place. This may sound like a semantic game, but the order is vitally important. If discipleship depends upon my obedience, then the primary focus of Jesus' statement is on my ability to comply with all that God commands. If, on the other hand, obedience depends upon the reality of my discipleship relationship with Jesus Christ, the primary focus is on Christ Himself. In John 8:31–32 discipleship comes before obedience. Obedience is the consequence, not the cause.

Rooted in God's Grace

The Scriptures speak of two very different kinds of obedience. One could be called "legalistic" obedience. The other might be described as "grace-rooted" obedience. Legalistic obedience is rooted in human effort and achievement—obeying God's commands in order to earn a righteous standing in God's sight. In Paul's day those who depended upon religious rituals to make themselves right with God epitomized this kind of obedience. It is the polar opposite of grace-rooted obedience (Galatians 5:3–4). The objective in legalistic obedience may seem like a good one—the observance of God's commands—but it is flawed because it overestimates the human capacity to comply. It produces an obedience that is grounded in self rather than in God.

Grace, like legalism, also has obedience to God's commands as its objective. According to Romans 2:14, it is not those who hear God's Law who are declared righteous but those who obey it. But the difference with obedience that's rooted in grace is that it is grounded in Christ's righteousness rather than my own. It is "the obedience that comes from faith" (Romans 1:5). For the Christian, faith *is* obedience because it focuses on the one who obeyed all God's commands on my behalf. When I trust in Jesus Christ, my faith is credited to me as righteousness (Romans 4:5). Grace-rooted obedience recognizes that righteousness can only be received as a gift. It cannot be earned as a wage. My obedience is an expression of gratitude for that gift.

It is not surprising, then, that Jesus repeatedly identified love as the primary motive for obedience. "If you love me," He told His disciples, "you will obey what I command." "He who does not love me," He warned, "will not obey my teaching" (John 14:15, 24).

Rooted in Our Relationship with Jesus

There are other motives for obedience mentioned in Scripture that seem more "selfish." Grace-rooted obedience does not look for a wage, but it does expect to be rewarded. Yet even these rewards are ultimately rooted in our relationship to Jesus Christ. For example, Jesus promised those who kept His teaching that its truth would make them free (John 8:32). In the context of John's gospel, however, truth is not merely a set of propositions. Ultimately it is embodied in the person of Christ Himself. "I am the way and the truth and the life," Jesus declared. "No one comes to the Father except through me" (John 14:6). "The truth of which John writes," explained commentator Leon Morris, "is the truth that is bound up with the Person and work of Jesus."[6]

There is propositional content to the truth of Christ. Those who rejected Him rejected His teaching. Conversely, when Jesus said that those who held to His teaching would find the truth, ultimately He meant that they would find Him. They would enter into a relationship with the one who is truth. Those who believe in Jesus receive the person of Christ (John 1:12). "Jesus is clear that this truth, that truth that is the way and the life, is himself," William Willimon observed. "We really [would] have no idea what the truth is, living as we do in a culture of lies, had not Jesus shown us a life that is true to God."[7]

Likewise, the freedom spoken of in John 8:31–32 is not primarily a matter of social status. I find freedom in Christ who is the truth because I enter into an entirely new relationship with God, with His Law, and even with myself. Because Christ took upon Himself the curse that is the consequence of disobedience to God's Law, even though He Himself had never disobeyed it, I am free from that Law's penalty. I am no longer under what Paul called "the curse of the law" (Galatians 3:13). This blunt phrase is a forceful reminder of how desperate bondage to sin truly is. In itself God's Law is holy, righteous, and good (Romans 7:12). The Law's weakness is our sinful nature. The Law is spiritual; we are unspiritual, "sold as a slave to sin" (Romans 7:14). When God's Law comes into contact with our sinful condition, the result is toxic.

I recently read the news story of a woman who suffered from a food allergy so severe that if she were to eat certain foods like peanut butter, she would go into shock and eventually die. When her husband kissed her on the cheek after eating the same foods, her face broke out in welts. In her case, what was intended to nourish instead had the potential to kill. This is similar to the effect that God's Law has on the sinful nature. When it comes in contact with the Law, the sinful nature produces a desire for the very thing that God's Law forbids (Romans 7:8). Paul described the tragic result this way: "The very commandment that was intended to bring life actually brought death" (Romans 7:10).

Christ's death frees us from slavery to the sinful nature and gives us a new freedom to obey (John 8:34–36; Romans 6:18, 22).

Rooted in a Desire for Answered Prayer

Answered prayer is another motive for obedience in the Christian life. In 1 John 3:21–22 we seem to be promised unlimited answers to our prayers: "Dear friends, if our hearts do not condemn us, we have confidence before God and receive from him anything we ask, because we obey his commands and do what pleases him." J. C. Ryle echoed this verse when he observed, "The name of Jesus is a never-failing passport to our prayers. In that name a man may draw near to God with boldness and ask with confidence."[8]

However, although answers to prayer are indeed guaranteed in this passage, those answers are limited by several important qualifications. First, the promise is made to those who have a clear conscience. Only those whose "hearts do not condemn" them and who "have confidence before God" can be assured that they will receive anything they ask. Second, the promise is made to those who are in tune with God. They "obey His commands and do what pleases Him." It is no wonder, then, that their prayers are answered. It's not because they have earned the right to receive their requests from God, but because they know how to ask "according to his will" (1 John 5:14). In other words, the secret is in the relationship.

The Mark of Abiding Fruit

According to Jesus, prayer leads to personal transformation. Those who "abide" in Christ pray in a way that results in spiritual fruit. "If you remain in me and my words remain in you," Jesus said, "ask whatever you wish, and it will be given you. This is to my Father's glory, that you bear much fruit, showing yourselves to be my disciples" (John 15:7–8). Earlier, Jesus had compared His relationship with the disciples to that of a vine. "I am the vine; you are the branches. If a man remains in me and I in him, he will bear much fruit; apart from me you can do nothing" (John 15:5). Results are expected of the disciple, but they are the results of being connected to the vine. It is the life of the vine that generates the fruit.

What We Do

Yet there is clearly an element of personal responsibility involved in this. Believers are commanded to remain in the vine and to remain in Christ's love (John 15:4, 9). Jesus did not explain further what is meant by "abiding," but the context provides several clues.

First, those who abide recognize their dependency upon Christ. The command to abide is not a call to shift the focus from Christ to myself. Although the believer has the responsibility of abiding, it is not possible to produce fruit apart from Christ, who said, "Apart from me you can do nothing" (John 15:5). When I abide, I am conscious that everything Christ commands of me Christ must also produce in me. It is a state that might be described as "actively passive." It is both active and passive at the same time.

Second, those who abide recognize the importance of Scripture. Abiding in the vine means that I will allow Christ's Word to dwell in me. There is something more to this than a simple command to read the Bible. It is a command to allow Christ's Word to impact my life at its deepest level. To abide in Christ's Word is to know it and embrace it. Commentator Leon Morris noted that the language of abiding was used by the rabbis to speak of studying the Torah.[9] Christ's Word plays a critical role in spiritual growth because it contains promises and commands. The promises tell me what to expect of God, and the commands tell me what to expect of myself. In fact, these are related. Christ's commands are grounded in His promises to me.

Third, those who abide recognize their responsibility to pray. The connection between prayer and the fruit promised by Jesus further underscores the role that God plays in this process. If producing spiritual fruit were purely a matter of determined effort, there would be no need to "ask whatever you wish." Why ask God for what we alone can produce? The very fact that we must ask is an indication that fruit is something that can come only from God.

Fourth, those who abide recognize the need to grow further. Branches that produced grapes for only one season would not have been considered very fruitful. It is not merely fruitfulness that Christ desires but continuing fruitfulness. Fortunately for us, the Father is actively involved in making certain that those who have produced fruit will continue to do so. He "prunes" every branch so that it will be even more fruitful (John 15:2). Jesus does not elaborate on what is involved in the pruning process. The image of pruning itself suggests a cutting away of that which is unproductive or "dead" in the believer's life. The word that is translated "prune" in John 15:2 can also mean "cleanse." Jesus' assurance to the disciples that they had already been cleansed by His word (v. 3) points to that same word as the Father's main pruning agent.

What the Fruit Looks Like

Christ does not expect His disciples to bear a little fruit, but "much fruit," and He expects it to be "fruit that will last" (John 15:8, 16). But what does this spiritual fruit look like? Several lists are found elsewhere in Scripture. Paul described a list of character traits that he calls the "fruit of the Spirit" in Galatians 5:22–23 and the "fruit of the light" in Ephesians 5:9. Colossians 1:10 speaks of good works as a type of fruit, and the author of Hebrews calls worship "the fruit of lips that confess his name" (Hebrews 13:15). James wrote that the wisdom that comes from heaven as a gift to all who ask is "full of mercy and good fruit" (James 3:17).

In the context of John 15, however, Jesus emphasizes the importance of the fruit of love (v. 12). Love is so important that elsewhere Jesus identifies it as the one mark that will convince the world that we are genuine disciples. "Love one another. As I have loved you, so you must love one another. By this all men will know that you are my disciples, if you love one another" (John 13:34–35).

THE MARK OF LOVE

Francis Schaeffer called love "the mark of a Christian" and said that it is the church's final apologetic before a watching world. "Jesus is giving a right to the world," he wrote. "Upon his authority he gives the world the right to judge whether you and I are born-again Christians on the basis of our observable love toward all Christians."[10] Our obligation, of course, is not limited exclusively to Christians (Mark 12:28–31; Luke 10:27). Christ has commanded us to love everyone, whether they are believers or not. But there is a special obligation when it comes to other believers. We are to "do good to all people, [but] especially to those who belong to the family of believers" (Galatians 6:10).

The Origin of Our Love

The apostle John identified love as the distinguishing mark of those who know God (1 John 4:7–8). His argument was simple. If love has its origin in God, then we ought to love because we have our origin in God. If we belong to Him, we ought, in some measure, to be like Him.

Lovers often adopt the same interests. When a man who can't tell a French horn from a piano falls in love with someone who is fond of classical music, he may find that he suddenly wants tickets to the symphony. It is one of the characteristics of love. If the one I love is interested in something, I will cultivate an interest in the same thing. People who have been married for a long time often begin to talk like one another. Some even begin to resemble each other physically.

The same principle holds true in our relationship with God. If we love God, we will want to be like Him. We will love what God loves. This would be easy if those whom God loves were always lovable. Unfortunately, He has a penchant for loving the unlovely and for setting His affection on those who don't love Him back. We shouldn't be surprised. This was our own experience. "We love him, because he first loved us" (1 John 4:19 KJV).

Our obligation to love as Christ loves is further challenged by today's confused notions about the nature of love. We talk about "falling in love" as if it were some kind of a ditch that we stumbled into. Husbands and wives break their marriage vows because they "love" someone else. People who commit sexual immorality say that they are "making love." If we are to bear the identifying mark of love, we had better know what true love is like.

True Biblical Love

Biblical love is active. It is reflected more in what we do than in how we feel. Today's society views love primarily as an emotion. Although emotion plays a part, its role is secondary. In this respect, love is much like faith. C. S. Lewis has defined faith as "the art of holding on to things your reason has once accepted in spite of your changing moods."[11] Moods change so that what seemed likely one day looks improbable the next. The role of faith, Lewis argued, is to tell your moods "where they get off."[12] Moods also change with regard to people. I can feel affectionate toward someone today and cold toward the same person tomorrow. Like faith, there are times when love needs to tell my emotions where to "get off." Love, like faith, involves an exercise of the will.

True love isn't necessarily feeling good about another person. It is acting towards them in a way that is pleasing to God and appropriate to their need.

It is possible to feel powerful emotion for the brother or sister who is in need and still refuse to help him or her, even though I have the means. In such a case all I have experienced is an empty emotion. In fact, according to James, such behavior isn't just an expression of false love; ultimately it is false faith. "Suppose a brother or sister is without clothes and daily food," he wrote. "If one of you says to him, 'Go, I wish you well; keep warm and well fed,' but does nothing about his physical needs, what good is it? In the same way, faith by itself, if it is not accompanied by action, is dead" (James 2:15–17). Similarly, John warned that anyone who has material possessions and sees his brother in need but has no pity on him, does not have the love of God in him.

Our love is to go beyond words. We are to "love . . . with actions and in truth" (1 John 3:18). If love is ultimately my commitment to act in a loving way toward another, it is possible for me to show love toward someone even when my feelings haven't quite caught up with my commitment. This doesn't mean that we should be satisfied with love that is cold and calculating. According to 1 Peter 1:22, we are to "love one another deeply, from the heart." A church where the prevailing spirit says, "I love you but I don't really like you" is unlikely to have much of an impact on the world.

Biblical love is also inclusive. It is open to those who are unlike it. Nowhere is this seen more vividly than in the church. Christ often brings together unlikely people. We can see this in Jesus' own disciples: a fisherman, a revolutionary, a doctor, a government minion. One wonders how they all got along with each other. The truth is, they didn't. Sometimes they got on one another's nerves. They argued and tried to outdo each other (Mark 9:34). They even criticized Jesus at times (Matthew 26:8–9). Yet through it all Jesus repeatedly called them back to this command: "Love one another."

Love That Grows

Biblical love is expansive. It is a love that grows. In 1 John 4:17 the apostle spoke of the need for love to be "made complete" in us. The idea conveyed in the original text is that love will be brought to full measure.

But how does this take place? John explains that it comes about when we live in God's love: "And so we know and rely on the love God has for us. God is love. Whoever lives in love lives in God, and God in him. In this way, love is made complete among us so that we will have confidence on the day of judgment, because in this world we are like him" (1 John 4:16–17). The secret is not in trying harder. It is in living closer. The way to grow in love is to live in God's love.

The love that Christ commands me to have is the same love that I have experienced. That is why it is such an important evidence of true faith.

A REALITY CHECK

Discipleship is faith expressed in practice. But there is far more to it than merely watching your language on the loading dock. At its heart, it is a living relationship with the Christ we love, serve, and seek to imitate. For many, if not all of us, however, there is room for considerable improvement. Merely cosmetic changes will not help us. Christ is not calling us to put on appearances. Neither should we deny the depth of our problem.

Our best hope is to take a good hard look at ourselves and determine which of the marks of discipleship are missing. If having a relationship with Christ is the key to being a true disciple, repentance is always the first step in that relationship.

THE COST OF DISCIPLESHIP

TAKING UP THE CROSS

Most churches have at least one. Some are simple wooden things, rough-hewn and unadorned. Others are more ornate, made of steel, marble, or even neon. They can be mounted on the wall, placed on an altar, or set high atop a steeple.

The cross is the most recognizable symbol of the Christian faith. We preach about it, sing about it, and even wear it as an item of jewelry. Of all the images Jesus used when calling His disciples to commitment, none was more powerful than the image of the cross. He warned His disciples that "anyone [who] would come after me . . . must deny himself and take up his cross daily and follow me" (Luke 9:23).

If the message of the Cross is at the center of the Christian faith, it is the life of the Cross that is at the heart of Christian discipleship. Its popularity as a Christian symbol and our overfamiliarity with Jesus' command have resulted in a romanticized view of the Cross. Yet Christ's own disciples did not at first understand the importance of the cross in Jesus' ministry or its role in their own discipleship experience.

CALLS TO TAKE UP THE CROSS

The First Call

Jesus appears to have issued the command to take up the cross on at least three primary occasions. One was when Jesus sent the Twelve out to preach throughout Judea. This initial mission was much more limited in scope (Matthew 10:5–6) than the commission Jesus would give to the disciples after His resurrection. Both commissions, however, would provoke the same reaction. Some would accept the message gladly and become disciples themselves. Others would reject the gospel and oppose those who preached it.

Jesus warned that in some cases His disciples would find that their closest relatives had become their worst enemies (Matthew 10:17–18, 21–22, 34–36). It was in this context that He warned: "Anyone who loves his father or mother more than me is not worthy of me; anyone who loves his son or daughter more than me is not worthy of me; and anyone who does not take his cross and follow me is not worthy of me" (Matthew 10:37–38).

The Second Call

Another occasion when Jesus called His followers to take up the cross is found in Luke 14:26–27. Although its similar language may mean that it is identical with the one recorded in Matthew 10:38, there are some significant differences. In Matthew 10:38 the charge is made to the Twelve. In Luke's account, the saying is addressed to the large crowd that was following Jesus. The language of Luke's parallel is slightly stronger than Matthew's: "If anyone comes to me and does not hate his father and mother, his wife and children, his brothers and sisters—yes, even his own life—he cannot be my disciple. And anyone who does not carry his cross and follow me cannot be my disciple." This does not mean that we regard our parents, brothers and sisters, or spouse as unimportant. We continue to have an obligation to love and respect them. The "hatred" spoken of in this passage is by way of comparison. It is hyperbolic language meant to drive home our obligation to love Christ more than any other and to defer to Him in all our decisions.

The command to take up the cross involves a personal commitment to Jesus Christ that takes precedence over everything else. It calls us to cherish Christ more than any other human bond. As New Testament scholar F. F. Bruce explained, "The interests of God's kingdom must be paramount with the followers of Jesus, and everything else must take second place to them, even family ties."[1]

Family members may not understand or even approve of your commitment to Christ. They may be disappointed with your choices and disagree with your priorities. While you must not be callous toward them, neither should you let their opinion alter your decision to choose the way of the Cross. Even Jesus experienced similar misunderstandings with those in His human family (Mark 3:21).

Luke's account of the call to take up the cross is also coupled with a warning to count the cost of discipleship. Jesus compared the disciple to a man who builds a tower or a king who plans to go to war with another king (see Luke 14:28–32). Both would estimate the potential cost of such a project before embarking on it. Those who answer the call to discipleship must do so thoughtfully. Christ is not looking for rash decisions that are made in the heat of the moment and then easily abandoned. Those who answer the call must know what Christ requires—He asks for everything. "In the same way," Jesus warned, "any of you who does not give up everything he has cannot be my disciple" (v. 33). But when He said this, did He really mean to imply that we can "pay" the cost of discipleship? The examples Jesus used suggest that we cannot.

The danger for the man who builds the tower is that he may lay the foundation and not be able to finish it (vv. 29–30). The king described in Jesus' example only has an army of ten thousand and is contemplating battle with an army of twenty thousand.

The implication is clear. Those who count the cost will realize that they do not have the resources in themselves to be faithful. C. S. Lewis quoted fantasy writer George MacDonald when he said that "God is easy to please, but hard to satisfy."[2] Jesus demands far more than our best effort. He is not satisfied with anything less than "everything." His goal for us, although it will not be fully realized until eternity, is nothing short of perfection. "To shrink back from that plan is not humility;" warned Lewis, "it is laziness and cowardice. To submit to it is not conceit or megalomania; it is obedience."[3]

The Third Call

The third time that Jesus issued the command to carry the cross was when He revealed to the Twelve that He would go to Jerusalem and there be killed. Deeply troubled by this, Peter took Jesus aside and began to rebuke Him (Matthew 16:22). Jesus' response was as blunt as it was swift: "Jesus turned and said to Peter, 'Get behind me, Satan! You are a stumbling block to me; you do not have in mind the things of God, but the things of men.'" (v. 23). Then Jesus addressed the disciples and said, "If anyone would come after me, he must deny himself and take up his cross and follow me" (v. 24; cf. Mark 8:34; Luke 9:23).

On the previous occasion Jesus had warned that discipleship might mean that those who follow Him will be disowned by those who are closest to them. Here Jesus revealed that it would mean breaking ties on an even more intimate level. Being a disciple is fundamentally a matter of denying self. The Greek term that is translated "deny" means to renounce a claim on something. This is a choice I make. I do not have any control over whether my family members disown me. I do choose whether I will have more regard for "the things of men" than for the things of God.

Ironically, saying no to self is also the safest form of self-interest. Jesus warned that the one who tries to save his life will lose it and promised that those who would lose their life for His sake will find it (Matthew 16:25).

"Must Jesus bear the cross alone, and all the world go free?" asks the old hymn. "No," the hymn writer replies, "there's a cross for everyone, and there's a cross for me."[4] We don't hear these words sung much in the church today. Perhaps that is because we think its message is not upbeat enough for modern audiences. Yet Jesus makes it clear that every disciple must bear the cross.

In the Roman world, the cross was an instrument of torture and execution. It was a symbol of shame (Hebrews 12:2). When Jesus called upon those who would follow Him to take up their own cross, He gave notice that the disciple's lot would be one of self-denial and death to the old nature. Most of the apostles eventually suffered martyrdom as a result of their commitment to Christ, but the kind of cross-bearing that is commanded of all disciples is more enduring. It is not a single event but something that Christ calls us to practice every day.

There is another more personal aspect to cross-bearing. It is the practice some of the older theologians refer to as "mortification." Mortification is the believer's intentional effort to say no to the desires of the flesh on a daily basis.

THE LIVING DEAD

Sherwin Nuland was a third-year medical student when he saw James McCarty die. McCarty had been admitted because of chest pains earlier in the day to the hospital where Nuland was being trained. Only minutes after Nuland had entered McCarty's room to get his medical history, the patient threw back his head and gasped. He turned a ghastly shade of purple, struck the front of his chest with his balled fists, and died right in front of Nuland's eyes.

Nuland shouted for help, but no one could hear him. He placed his hand on McCarty's neck but did not find a pulse. CPR was an unknown procedure at the time, so Nuland did the only thing he knew how to do. In desperation he grabbed a nearby scalpel, cut into McCarty's breastbone and gently took the man's arrested heart into his bare hands. Nuland then began to massage the heart in an attempt to keep blood flowing to the brain until help arrived and they could shock the heart back into operation. He could tell, however, by the way the heart was responding, that it wasn't filling with blood. The patient was beyond help.

Still, Nuland persisted. "And suddenly," Nuland writes, "something stupefying in its horror took place—the dead McCarty, whose soul was by that time totally departed, threw back his head once more and, staring upward at the ceiling with the glassy, unseeing gaze of open dead eyes, roared out to the distant heavens a dreadful rasping whoop, that sounded like the hounds of hell were barking."5

Nuland's experience may have been horrifying, but it was not unique. We usually think of death as the cessation of physical activity. Yet it is not unusual for a corpse in its final moments to heave, twitch, or even experience a convulsion. Sometimes referred to as the "agonal phase" of death, Nuland writes that this final struggle of the body is "like some violent outburst of protest arising deep in the primitive unconscious, raging against the too-hasty departure of the spirit."6

THE STRUGGLE CONTINUES

The same might be said of the believer's sinful nature. Although it has been dealt a deathblow by the work of Christ, one from which it will never recover, it continues to struggle to assert itself. The apostle Paul describes his own personal conflict with the presence of sin in these vivid words: "For what I do is not the good I want to do; no, the evil I do not want to do—this I keep on doing. Now if I do what I do not want to do, it is no longer I who do it, but it is sin living in me that does it. So I find this law at work: When I want to do good, evil is right there with me" (Romans 7:19–21).

In a way, this confession should surprise us. After all, it is also Paul who writes that our "old self was crucified with [Christ] so that the body of sin might be done away with, that we should no longer be slaves to sin" (Romans 6:6). He said that those who belong to Jesus Christ have been crucified with Christ (Galatians 2:20). He also said that those who belong to Christ have crucified the sinful nature (Galatians 5:24). They have "put off" the sinful nature and have been "buried" with Christ in baptism (Colossians 2:11–12). If we have truly died to sin, then, why does it still seem so alive? How is it possible that, like Paul, when we want to do good we find that evil is still "right there" with us?

The answer is that our new position in Christ has freed us from sin's domination but not from sin's influence. The sinful nature has been crucified with Christ, but it has not been eliminated. To use Paul's language, although I am no longer living in sin, sin continues to "live" in me. Sin is still a presence in the believer's life. It may, indeed, be in its death throes. But like the death throes of the human body, sin's final struggle can be horrifying both in scope and power. Consequently, when Paul described believers as those who "have crucified the sinful nature with its passions and desires" (Galatians 5:24), he did not mean that once someone trusts in Christ the flesh disappears. It is at that point that the struggle really begins. To understand why this would be the case, it is necessary to know something about the believer's spiritual condition prior to Jesus Christ.

OUR PREVIOUS CONDITION

Prior to faith in Christ, all believers were spiritually dead. Paul described this condition in Ephesians 2:1–3: "As for you, you were dead in your transgressions and sins, in which you used to live when you followed the ways of this world and of the ruler of the kingdom of the air, the spirit who is now at work in those who are disobedient." Recalling their activities at that time, Paul added, "All of us also lived among them at one time, gratifying the cravings of our sinful nature and following its desires and thoughts. Like the rest, we were by nature objects of wrath."

These verses reveal several important characteristics of spiritual death. The most striking is that those who are spiritually dead are quite active physically, socially, and intellectually. They are the "living dead." They live (or, in the King James Version, "walk") in their transgressions and sins. This means that they are in a state of rebellion against God and are automatically inclined to follow a path that is opposed to His rule. They are one-sided as far as their nature goes. Everything the spiritually dead do can serve only to gratify the cravings of the sinful nature in thought and deed. They have no other capacity.

This may sound as though their lives were marked by a continual orgy, and in some cases this might be true, but the flesh also has many "respectable" avenues in which to manifest itself. Pride, selfish ambition, and jealousy are as much expressions of the sinful nature as are drunkenness and sexual immorality (Galatians 5:17–21). Even religious zeal, when it is not rooted in the grace of God that comes through Jesus Christ, is an expression of the flesh, Paul explained, citing himself as an example (Philippians 3:3–9). As John Stott has warned, "Wherever 'self' rears its ugly head against God or man, there is 'the flesh.'"[7]

If this is the constant state of all those who are outside Christ, Paul is also clear that it is the former state of all those who are now a part of Christ. We who were once dead in trespasses and sins have been "made alive" in Christ (Ephesians 2:5). All that Paul says about what it means to be dead in transgressions and sins is ancient history to the believer. It describes what we once were, not what we are. Most importantly, it means that we are no longer dead. When we were unable to help ourselves, God intervened and gave us spiritual life. He changed our status by making us His children and transformed our nature when He "raised us up with Christ and seated us with him in the heavenly realms in Christ Jesus" (Ephesians 2:6).

If those who have never placed their faith in Jesus Christ are the living dead because they live in a state of spiritual death, then we who are in Christ are the living dead in an entirely different sense. We are alive to God and have died to sin (Romans 6:2, 11).

FREEDOM FROM SIN

However, given the continuing presence of sin in the believer's life, to what extent are we really "free" from sin? The Scriptures outline three major areas of freedom.

First, we are free from the guilt of sin. The guilt that should have been ours has been transferred to Christ: "God made him who had no sin to be sin for us, so that in him we might become the righteousness of God" (2 Corinthians 5:21).

Second, we are free from the divine wrath that is the natural consequence of sin. The Scriptures frequently warn that the deeds of the sinful nature provoke God to anger (Romans 2:8; Ephesians 5:6; Colossians 3:6). Jesus is called the one "who rescues us from the coming wrath" (1 Thessalonians 1:10). Because His death and resurrection have made us righteous in God's sight, we will be spared the wrath that is to come (Romans 5:9).

But Jesus has done more than give us positional freedom from sin. We also enjoy freedom in a very practical sense. We may not be free from sin's presence, but we have been freed from its power. Sin is no longer the ruling force in the believer's life. That is why Paul urges us to count ourselves dead to sin: "Therefore do not let sin reign in your mortal body so that you obey its evil desires. Do not offer the parts of your body to sin, as instruments of wickedness, but rather offer yourselves to God, as those who have been brought from death to life; and offer the parts of your body to him as instruments of righteousness" (Romans 6:12–13).

So, third, we are free from sin's power to rule our lives. An entirely new potential has opened up to us. It is the possibility of saying yes to God and no to the flesh. This blessing brings with it an inevitable responsibility. Since there are now two ways open to the believer—the possibility of saying yes to God or of acting according to the old nature—we have the responsibility of applying the work of the Cross to the flesh. Consequently, Paul not only says that believers have already crucified the sinful nature, he commands them to "put to death" the flesh in their present experience: "Put to death, therefore, whatever belongs to your earthly nature: sexual immorality, impurity, lust, evil desires and greed, which is idolatry" (Colossians 3:5; cf. Romans 8:13–14).

The sinful nature can be "put to death," but it cannot be changed. It will never be capable of pleasing God. The sinful nature is incapable of submitting to God or of pleasing Him (Romans 8:6–8). The only way to defeat the continuing presence of sin is to take up the cross.

HANDLING TEMPTATION

Using Prayer

Although the presence of the sinful nature makes temptation a very real threat to the Christian, we can take practical steps to deal with it. One of the most effective is to be proactive. We do not need to wait until we are in the midst of temptation before setting up safeguards. The best way to cope with temptation is to avoid it altogether. The Scriptures prescribe two basic strategies for doing this. One strategy is to pray that we will not come to the place of temptation. In the Lord's Prayer, Jesus taught His disciples to pray, "Lead us not into temptation, but deliver us from the evil one" (Matthew 6:13).

At first glance, the language of this petition might seem troubling, because it could imply that God sometimes leads us into temptation. Yet James 1:13–14 assures us that the temptation to sin never originates with God: "When tempted, no one should say, 'God is tempting me.' For God cannot be tempted by evil, nor does he tempt anyone; but each one is tempted when, by his own evil desire, he is dragged away and enticed." Some Bible scholars believe that the Greek term translated "temptation" in the Lord's prayer actually refers to trials or testing.[8] The companion request, however, supports translating the term as "temptation," because it suggests that the context of the petition is one of deliverance from evil. God is incapable of tempting us, but He is powerful enough to protect us from temptation's allure. When we pray this, we are not asking Him to set limits on Himself but to set limits on us. We are asking God to protect us from the circumstances of temptation and from the potential of succumbing to the evil desires that arise within our own hearts.[9]

On the night of His betrayal and arrest, Jesus found the disciples sleeping in the garden while He agonized in prayer. Not long before this, He had warned His disciples that they would soon abandon Him. They did not believe Him but swore that they would follow Him to the point of death (Mark 14:27–31). Although they were sincere in their assertion, they had seriously underestimated their own weakness and the power of the temptation they were about to face. Finding them unprepared for what was going to take place, Jesus warned, "Watch and pray so that you will not fall into temptation. The spirit is willing, but the body is weak" (Matthew 26:41; Mark 14:38).

Martyn Lloyd-Jones has warned, "There are situations which will be dangerous to you; watch and pray, always be on guard lest you fall into temptation."[10] Prayer has the power to protect us from ever having to face such harmful temptations.

Avoiding Temptations

To deal with sin proactively, your prayers should be coupled with the commonsense strategy of avoidance. In the Lord's Prayer, we pray that God will keep us from those circumstances of temptation that we do not know about. Sometimes, however, we knowingly place ourselves within the range of temptation. Avoiding temptation means that whenever possible we will keep away from those circumstances where we know we will be tempted.

Thus the second strategy is to be intentional in avoiding the people or places where we know we will be vulnerable. Or, in today's language, when it comes to temptation, "Don't go there!"

When others invite us to join them in sin, Proverbs 1:15 advises, "Do not go along with them, do not set foot on their paths." To accomplish this we may need to replace old interests or friends with new ones. One man I know was an avid golfer and earned his living as a golf pro. Although there was nothing inherently sinful in either of these things, after becoming a Christian, he realized that the lifestyle associated with them was exposing him to a level of temptation that was hurting his spiritual life. To protect himself, he left his old profession and started a new business. Obviously, choices like this must be weighed individually. Other Christians might have continued in the same profession without being troubled by the environment. For my friend, however, the safest course of action was to avoid the temptation altogether.

But can temptation always be avoided? Jesus indicated that some of the things that cause people to sin are inevitable (Matthew 18:7).

Likewise, the apostle Paul said that the temptations we experience are "common to man" (1 Corinthians 10:13). This was not intended to minimize the danger of temptation, but to keep us from concluding that our experience is unique. Otherwise we might decide that our situation is a special case and go down in defeat before the battle begins.

God does not tempt. Nor does He allow the believer to be tempted beyond his or her ability to bear it. Instead, He enables us to endure temptation by providing a way out. Your greatest weapons in the battle against sin may be your own two feet!

STAGES OF TEMPTATION

1. Desire

James identified three major stages in temptation. The first is the stage of desire (James 1:14). This is the stage when we feel the draw to sin on two fronts. We are drawn to it internally as we are "dragged away and enticed" by our own evil desire. But we also feel it externally as we are attracted to "the pleasures of sin" (Hebrews 11:25). At this point, although we are attracted to it, we have not acted upon the desire. Like the fisherman's bait that hides the sharp barb of the hook, the attractiveness of sin masks the ultimate disappointment and eventual bondage that is its result.

Sin always promises more than it can deliver. For proof, we need only look at the first instance of temptation in the Garden of Eden. Satan promised Eve that if she ate the fruit, she would "be like God, knowing good and evil" (Genesis 3:5). This appeal to sin was further strengthened by the fact that it was rooted in legitimate desires and normal appetites. The fruit of the forbidden tree was attractive because it was good for food, pleasing to the eye, and eating it seemed to be a way to obtain wisdom. Not one of these is bad in the appropriate context. Even the desire to be like God was ultimately a good one. It was God's intent all along for us (Matthew 5:48; Luke 6:36). Deceived by these false promises, however, Eve lost sight of God's warning that disobedience would result in death.

The stage of desire is the point when we need to look beyond the initial false promises of temptation and ask ourselves some important questions. If the appeal of sin is rooted in normal desires, what legitimate means has God provided for seeing that those desires are fulfilled? Moreover, how will taking the illegitimate shortcut of sin now spoil our legitimate enjoyment later on? How will we view the temptation after we have experienced the shame and guilt that will be its result?

2. Conception

James described the second stage of temptation as conception: "Then, after desire has conceived, it gives birth to sin" (James 1:15a). During the conception stage, it is not unusual to begin to rationalize the decision to sin. We may reason, for example, that what we are contemplating is only a "small" sin. Of course, there is no such thing.

How great was Moses' sin when he struck the rock instead of speaking to it? To us it seems like a small thing, but in God's eyes it was a failure to honor Him as holy (Numbers 20:8–12). Uzzah's sin must also have seemed insignificant. He merely reached out to steady the ark of the covenant when it seemed about to topple from the cart that was transporting it to Jerusalem. Yet 1 Chronicles 13:10 says: "The Lord's anger burned against Uzzah, and he struck him down because he had put his hand on the ark. So he died there before God." All Ananias and Sapphira did was fudge in their accounting to God. They sold a piece of property, kept back part of it for themselves and gave the rest to the church—leaving everyone with the impression that they had given all the proceeds to God. We might think that God should at least have been satisfied with the fact that they had given some of their profit to Him. Yet from the Lord's perspective, the sin was much greater. They had lied to the Holy Spirit and were struck dead as a result (Acts 5:1–11).

There are no "little" sins. When it comes to God's Law, it only takes offending at one point to make us guilty of breaking it all (James 2:10). Our smallest sin was enough to require Christ to suffer and die.

3. Development and Bondage

Once sin has been born, it is not finished. The final stage is one of development and eventual bondage: "Sin, when it is full-grown, gives birth to death" (James 1:15b). Certainly physical death is part of what James has in mind. However, as we have seen, the biblical concept of spiritual death encompasses much more. Sin leads to slavery.

"Don't you know," Paul warned, "that when you offer yourselves to someone to obey him as slaves, you are slaves to the one whom you obey—whether you are slaves to sin, which leads to death, or to obedience, which leads to righteousness?" (Romans 6:16). Today's "little" sin paves the way for tomorrow's bondage. It may be conceived in momentary pleasure, but it will produce a harvest of regret. What began as an occasional "mistake" quickly develops into a practice. That practice eventually becomes a habit of life.

Why do some who profess to be Christ's disciples live as though they are slaves to sin? It is not because they have to. In fact, they are commanded not to. It is because they offer themselves to the flesh in voluntary slavery. It is time for them to discover that they have been serving a corpse.

THE POWER OF THE CROSS

"From the day of Christ's crucifixion," Horatius Bonar wrote, "the cross became a power in the earth which went forth like the light, noiselessly yet irresistibly—smiting down all religions alike, all shrines alike, all altars alike; sparing no superstition or philosophy; neither flattering priesthood nor succumbing to statesmanship; tolerating no error, yet refusing to draw the sword for truth; a power superhuman, yet wielded by human, not angelic hands; 'the power of God unto salvation.'"[11]

All who would be Christ's disciples must bear the cross. Yet all who do, find to their eternal joy that it is really the cross that bears them.

THE OBLIGATIONS OF DISCIPLESHIP

FOLLOWING CHRIST'S EXAMPLE

Dallas Willard was already a committed follower of Christ when he realized that he wasn't really trying to live like Jesus. This recognition came to him as he thought about his next-door neighbors, ex-bikers who made their living selling drugs. "As I brooded over them one day, indulging my irritation," Willard explained, "the Lord helped me see that I really had no love for them at all, that after 'suffering' from them for several years I would secretly be happy if they died so that we could just be rid of them."[1]

The experience disturbed Willard so much that it forced him to reexamine what the Gospels had to say about following Christ. "It is possible, I now believe, to 'put on the Lord Jesus Christ' (Romans 13:14 NASB)," he concluded. "Ordinary people in common surroundings can live from the abundance of God's kingdom, letting the spirit and the actions of Jesus be the natural outflow from their lives."[2]

JESUS, OUR EXAMPLE

Jesus is our Savior, but He is also our example. The desire to avoid a works-oriented approach to the Christian life has caused many evangelicals to ignore Christ's role as a model for the believer. Instead of trying to be like Jesus, we have adopted a far more modest goal. We are content to be "sort of" like Jesus. We hold Christ's life as a beautiful but unrealistic ideal. In fact, if another believer were to tell us that he or she actually lived like Christ, we would suspect that he or she was either exaggerating or conclude that the person had a serious problem with spiritual pride. We want to be like Jesus, but we do not think that it is really possible.

Yet Jesus taught that those who were genuinely interested in being His disciples would follow His example. "A student is not above his teacher, but everyone who is fully trained will be like his teacher," He said (Luke 6:40). The Greek term that is translated "fully trained" in this verse was used in other Greek writings to speak of preparing something or making it ready for use. It is the same term used in Mark 1:19 to describe the disciples' work of preparing the nets for the next day's fishing. Followers of Christ who are fully prepared are like Christ.

NOT "MEASURING UP" BUT "WORKING OUT"

But how realistic is such a goal? Puritan writer John Flavel admitted that taking Christ as our example would inevitably make us aware that we have fallen short of the very ideal we have adopted. "The imitation of Christ necessarily implies the imperfection of the best men in this life," he wrote. "For if the life of Christ be our pattern, the holiest men must confess they come short in every thing of the rule of their duty. Our pattern is still above us; the best of men are ashamed when they compare their lives to the life of Christ."[3]

This sounds like a contradiction. How can Christ's life be our pattern if it only serves to show us that we cannot meet the standard? The answer is to recognize that the disciples' goal is not to "measure up" to the life of Christ but to "work out" the reality of the Christ who lives in us (Philippians 2:12–13). This standard is not something outside of us; it is a principle that resides within. It is "Christ in you, the hope of glory" (Colossians 1:27). There is effort involved, but it is an effort that has been energized by the life of Christ (Colossians 1:29).

The apostle Paul's own practice of imitating Christ was rooted in his confidence that God was already at work in him. He was not trying to "catch up" to Christ but had himself already been "taken hold of" by Christ: "Not that I have already obtained all this, or have already been made perfect, but I press on to take hold of that for which Christ Jesus took hold of me. Brothers, I do not consider myself yet to have taken hold of it." Then he explained the goal: "But one thing I do: Forgetting what is behind and straining toward what is ahead, I press on toward the goal to win the prize for which God has called me heavenward in Christ Jesus" (Philippians 3:12–14). The responsibility is ours but the power to comply comes from God.

TRAINING IN CHRISTLIKENESS

God's standard for the disciple's life, then, is no less than Christ. He is the mark by which our spiritual maturity is measured and the aim of all our training. The reason that God has given believers spiritual gifts is to build the church up "until we all reach unity in the faith and in the knowledge of the Son of God and become mature, attaining to the whole measure of the fullness of Christ" (Ephesians 4:13). Our ultimate hope as believers is that we will one day be like Christ.

"Dear friends, now we are children of God, and what we will be has not yet been made known. But we know that when he appears, we shall be like him, for we shall see him as he is" (1 John 3:2). According to this verse, we must wait until Christ appears to be fully like Him. But this does not mean that we should wait until then before expecting to see a resemblance. In the same epistle, John points out that there is a correlation between our Christlikeness in the present and our assurance on the Day of Judgment: "In this way, love is made complete among us so that we will have confidence on the day of judgment, because in this world we are like him" (1 John 4:17).

The discipleship experience is training in Christlikeness. This is not merely a matter of asking ourselves, "What would Jesus do?" Our imitation of Christ begins with the mind and heart. We want to think like Christ as well as to act like Christ. "Your attitude," Paul admonishes, "should be the same as that of Christ Jesus: Who, being in very nature God, did not consider equality with God something to be grasped" (Philippians 2:5–6). The imitation of Christ begins, then, with an attitude of humility.

THE OBLIGATION OF HUMILITY

Humility is an essential precondition for discipleship, because a disciple ultimately is one who is under the yoke of Christ (Matthew 11:28–30). Unfortunately, humility is not highly valued, even by many Christians. Today's culture favors pride, which is considered to be an asset rather than a liability. Author and pastor Eugene Peterson notes: "It is difficult to recognize pride as a sin when it is held up on every side as a virtue, urged as profitable, and rewarded as an achievement."4 If humility is appreciated at all, it tends to be admired from a distance. We may approve of another's humility but do not often seek it for ourselves.

Yet the follower of Christ is told to "do nothing out of selfish ambition or vain conceit, but in humility consider others better than yourselves. Each of you should look not only to your own interests, but also to the interests of others" (Philippians 2:3–4).

TRUE VERSUS FALSE HUMILITY

Paul's command is troubling to some because it seems to say that we must run ourselves down in order to be humble; we are to consider everyone else to be better than we are. Is a low self-image the key to biblical humility? Not really. False humility is also a form of pride. The person who is always hanging his head and has nothing good to say about himself is usually more prideful than the person who graciously accepts a compliment. "False humility," Os Guinness has warned, "is actually self-driven and self-absorbed. A person who is falsely humble is a person who is truly proud."5

So how do we tell the difference between true and false humility? False humility will be marked by the two characteristics of pride mentioned in Philippians 2:3–4. The first is something the apostle calls "selfish ambition." This is the desire to advance my own interests at the expense of others. It is the competitive spirit twisted by the self-absorption of the sinful nature. Selfish ambition is listed among the works of the flesh in Galatians 5:20. It is reflected in false humility as a low estimate of myself that is driven by a selfish agenda. This is usually an attempt to elicit praise for a humility that does not exist or to prompt others to compliment me in the area of my affected humility. It is really a form of manipulation.

The other mark of pride that Paul identifies in Philippians 2:3–4 is "vain conceit." This is an attitude that is rooted in a false estimation of my position. It amounts to an empty boast. In false humility, this kind of conceit is reflected in the denial of real accomplishment or true ability. The person who achieves a difficult goal and then says that it was nothing is not humble. He or she is untruthful.

True humility is biblically informed realism. It is as likely to celebrate genuine strengths as it is to own up to real weaknesses. Consequently, the same Paul who claimed that he was "the least of the apostles" and did not deserve to be called an apostle, also admitted that he had "worked harder than all of them" (1 Corinthians 15:9–10). This was not an empty boast. He really had done so. It was also a claim that was coupled with this all-important qualifier: "yet not I, but the grace of God that was with me."

A WINSOME QUALITY

True humility is also focused on others. It does not neglect itself. It continues to look out for its own interests. But it is not willing to do so at the expense of others. It is equally interested in what others have done, desire, or need.

Few characteristics are as winsome as true biblical humility. That is why, according to C. S. Lewis, if we were to encounter biblical humility, we would be unlikely to recognize it. "Do not imagine that if you meet a really humble man he will be what most people call 'humble' nowadays: he will not be a sort of greasy, smarmy person, who is always telling you that, of course, he is nobody. Probably all you will think about him is that he seemed a cheerful, intelligent chap who took a real interest in what *you* said to *him*."[6]

It is said that when Queen Victoria lay dying, a member of the royal household wondered aloud whether she would be happy in heaven. "I don't know," the queen's son replied. "She will have to walk behind the angels—and she won't like that!" The test of true humility, however, does not lie in our ability to walk behind the angels so much as it does in our willingness to look out for the interests of others and to give place to them. It is not surprising, then, that along with humility another mark of the disciple is the willingness to submit.

THE OBLIGATION OF SUBMISSION

My twelve-year-old son was as annoyed with us as we were with him. With arms folded and eyes narrowed, he explained again why he thought we should let him spend the night at a friend's house. His other friends did it all the time. They weren't going to do anything bad. After all, what could possibly happen in the middle of the night? We repeated our reasons for refusing his request. We didn't know his friend's parents. We couldn't monitor what they might watch on television. For at least an hour we listed all the wise and loving parental concerns that had fueled our decision. He remained unconvinced and launched into his appeal again.

Finally my wife, Jane, cried out in exasperation, "Jarred, we aren't going to let you go! Why are you so determined to fight us on this?"

With the triumphant gleam of someone who is convinced that he has an irrefutable defense, he declared, "Because I don't like other people telling me what to do!"

I didn't know whether to laugh or cry. I was frustrated with his stubbornness, but I also knew exactly how he felt. I don't like other people telling me what to do, either. I don't know anyone who does. There is something about human nature that bristles at the thought of submission. Christ, however, was another matter. Although Jesus was equal with the Father, He did not cling to the rights and privileges of equality. He claimed, "I and the Father are one" (John 10:30). His enemies understood this to be a claim to deity (John 10:33). Yet He did not act on His own accord. He did only what He saw the Father doing (John 5:19). He said, "By myself I can do nothing; I judge only as I hear, and my judgment is just, for I seek not to please myself but him who sent me" (John 5:30).

The submission of Christ reached its peak in the Garden of Gethsemane. There He pleaded with the Father to let the cup of suffering pass from Him with the stipulation: "Yet not my will, but yours be done" (Luke 22:42).

If humility is low on society's wish list of character traits, the practice of submission is even lower. In an age of equal rights, the practice of submission has become synonymous with weakness and oppression. Christ's example, however, is proof that submission does not necessarily imply inferiority. When Jesus chose to submit to the Father's will, He was not any less the Son of God, nor was He any less equal with the Father in nature and power.

In the same way, when disciples follow Christ's pattern of submission, they are not any less than those to whom they submit. The fact that Ephesians 5:22 and Colossians 3:18 tell my wife to submit to my authority as a husband does not imply that Jane is inferior to me. As far as her position in Christ goes, she is my equal (Galatians 3:28). As far as her natural abilities are concerned, in many ways, she is my superior. My position as a leader in the home and hers as one who supports that leadership are differences of roles rather than of quality. Jane is not less than me if she submits, and I am not more than her if I exercise the responsibility of authority.

In the church's relationships, submission is more properly a gift to be offered than a right to be demanded. Although equal with the Father, Jesus did not cling to that equality. His submission was voluntary. He "made himself nothing" (Philippians 2:7). In the Incarnation,

Jesus "emptied" (NASB) or stripped Himself of the prerogatives that were His by virtue of His divine nature. He was not compelled to do this by the Father. He freely did so; during His earthly ministry Jesus took upon Himself the role of a servant rather than exercise His equality. According to the writer of Hebrews, He "learned obedience" during this period (Hebrews 5:8).

Although the Bible's teaching on submission has sometimes been used as a rationale for oppression and abuse, such behavior can never be legitimately validated by an appeal to biblical commands to submit. In the church and in the home, biblical authority must be recognized freely. It can never be seized.

The late Leonard Bernstein was once asked which musical instrument was the hardest to play. After considering the question for a moment, the composer and conductor replied, "The second fiddle. I can get plenty of first violinists, but to find someone who can play the second fiddle with enthusiasm—that's a problem. And if we have no second fiddle, we have no harmony." The same is true in the life of the church. What is needed today are more disciples willing to learn to play the second fiddle with enthusiasm.

THE OBLIGATION OF PATIENCE

Accepting the Weak

Another way disciples are to reflect Christ is by imitating His example of patience. More specifically, they are to bear with the limitations of the weak. "We who are strong ought to bear with the failings of the weak and not to please ourselves. Each of us should please his neighbor for his good, to build him up. For even Christ did not please himself but, as it is written: 'The insults of those who insult you have fallen on me.'" (Romans 15:1–3).

The "failings," or more literally "inabilities," that Paul refers to in this passage are probably the same matters of conscience described in the previous chapter of the epistle to the Romans. There Paul urged his readers to accept those whose faith was weak without passing judgment on them. The specific example he gave was of a person whose conscience permitted him to eat nothing but vegetables (Romans 14:2). Although he doesn't give the reason for such a conviction, it is likely that the vegetarianism of the "weaker" believer was for religious rather than health reasons. The problem may have been similar to the struggle in Corinth, where some of the church's members felt that they should not eat meat sold in the marketplace after it had been sacrificed to idols (1 Corinthians 8 and 10). Or the conscience of the "weak" believer may have been limited by convictions about clean and unclean foods and Sabbath observances (cf. Romans 14:5–6, 14). Either way, the obligation was the same. The strong were to "bear" or "carry" the weak. They were to shoulder the burden by considering the conviction of others first and not merely pleasing themselves.

Someone has called patience "the art of hoping." When it comes to exercising patience toward others, however, it might more accurately be described as "the art of enduring." In Ephesians 4:2 the apostle Paul urges believers to "be patient" by "bearing with one another in love." Together these phrases describe the two dimensions of patience. Internally, patience toward others requires self-control. The Greek word that is translated "patient" in Ephesians 4:2 conveys the idea of prolonged restraint of anger.[7] Externally, patience toward others demands forbearance. The Greek word that is translated "bearing with" one another in Ephesians 4:2 also means to "endure." It is the art of "putting up" with someone. These two practices are so related to each other that both words are virtually synonyms in the New Testament.

Prior to joining the faculty of the Moody Bible Institute, I served as a pastor. One afternoon as I was studying, Mike, one of the church's board members, burst into my office. I could tell that he was a man on a mission. "Did you notice Ed in church Sunday?" he asked. Ed taught one of the adult Sunday school classes.

"I saw that he was there," I answered, wondering where the conversation was headed.

"Well?" Mike demanded.

"Well what?" I replied.

"Didn't you notice that he was wearing an earring?" Mike asked.

I chuckled and shook my head. "Oh, yeah. Go figure!"

Ed had visited the local mall with his teenage son over the weekend. When his son decided to have one of his ears pierced, Ed decided, on a whim, to do the same. Now Mike, who couldn't understand how any self-respecting man (let alone a Sunday school teacher) could wear an earring, was demanding that the church do something about it. Did he have a point?

I opened my Bible to Romans 15:1–3 and asked Mike to read it: "We who are strong ought to bear with the failings of the weak and not to please ourselves. Each of us should please his neighbor for his good, to build him up. For even Christ did not please himself but, as it is written: 'The insults of those who insult you have fallen on me.'"

When Mike had finished, I asked, "Where do you and Ed fit into this passage? Which of you is 'strong' and which of you is 'weak?'"

Mike thought for a moment and with a sheepish smile said, "I'd have to say that I am the stronger. I'm probably the more mature between the two of us."

"Well, what does this passage tell you to do about it?" I asked.

He looked at the passage again and then spluttered, "But if what he's doing offends me, he's the one who is supposed to change, isn't he?"

I suggested that he read 1 Corinthians 8 and 10 and Romans 14 and 15 and then make an appointment with Ed to talk about it.

The next day Ed showed up at my door. He told me that Mike had visited him and said that he did not think Ed should teach a Sunday school class as long as he chose to wear an earring.

"What do you think about it?" I asked.

"I don't think he has the right to tell me how to dress!" Ed said defiantly. I asked him to read the same passages in Romans and Corinthians that I had given Mike. "Where do you and Mike fit into this passage? Which of you is 'strong' and which of you is 'weak?'"

Ed thought for a moment. "Mike would be the weaker, because it's his conscience that is bothered and not mine."

"So what does the passage tell you to do about it?" I asked.

"I guess I shouldn't wear the earring when Mike is around" he admitted.

In the end Mike and Ed agreed to disagree about the issue. Although he was not happy about Ed's choice, Mike reluctantly admitted that it was a matter of personal conscience, and Ed decided out of deference for Mike not to wear the earring while teaching.

Making Sacrifices for the Sake of the Weak

Yet how far should we go in allowing another's conviction to determine our behavior? Probably further than we would like. Paul writes, "It is better not to eat meat or drink wine or to do anything else that will cause your brother to fall" (Romans 14:21). This was Paul's personal practice. He was willing to give up meat permanently if it caused another believer to stumble (1 Corinthians 8:13).

There are, however, some important limitations when it comes to applying this principle. First, my decision to alter my behavior is not based upon another's personal taste alone. The command to bear with the weakness of others does not mean that we must gear our lives to the likes or dislikes of other believers. Suppose, for example, that you were to visit my home and sort through my CD collection. As you do, you notice that I have a CD by jazz trumpeter Miles Davis. You've heard Miles Davis before, and as far as you are concerned, his music is an ear-splitting cacophony of honks, snorts, and hoots. Am I obliged to throw out my CD because you don't like it? Certainly not—the fact that you dislike my music is irrelevant.

But let's take it a step further. Suppose you feel that my Miles Davis CD is the devil's music. You don't understand how any good Christian can listen to it, and you don't think that I should listen to it. Now what is my obligation? Obviously, I shouldn't put it on the stereo when you come over for a visit. In this case, the right course of action is described in Romans 14:22: "So whatever you believe about these things keep between yourself and God. Blessed is the man who does not condemn himself by what he approves." I should not try to impose my liberty on your conscience. However, by itself the fact that you think I am sinning by listening to jazz is not enough to compel me to change my behavior. The key question is not whether you like my actions or even whether you think I am sinning by them but whether my actions are causing you to sin. It is when my behavior causes you to violate your own conscience that I am obligated to limit myself.

There is clearly a cost involved in obeying this principle. In a way, both Mike and Ed paid a price when they decided to agree to disagree. Each had to allow personal preference to take a backseat to the preference of the other. This is what Jesus did. He "did not please Himself" (Romans 15:3).

"For His Good"

There is an important qualification added to the command of Romans 15:2. It says we are to please our neighbor "for his good." The goal is more than simply trying to please my neighbor. It is to please my neighbor in order to build him or her up in the faith.

In some cases, deferring to the conviction of another might not be in the person's best interest. It is clear, for example, that some believed that Paul was sinning by teaching that salvation came by grace alone apart from works. He refused to modify his message to suit their theology because he rightly judged that it would distort the gospel (Galatians 2:4–5). On another occasion Paul rebuked Peter publicly when he refused to eat with Gentile believers in Antioch. Peter had done this because of the conviction of some who had come from Jerusalem (Galatians 2:11–12). But Paul judged that Peter's behavior was "not . . . in line with the truth of the gospel" (Galatians 2:14).

Yet on other occasions Paul modified his behavior based upon the culture of those to whom he ministered (1 Corinthians 9:19–23). When Paul ministered to those who practiced the Law of Moses, he lived like a Jew and practiced Mosaic customs without altering his gospel. He observed the Law but did not preach that salvation came by the Law (1 Corinthians 9:20). When he ministered to the Gentiles, Paul lived like one who was free from the Law of Moses. At the same time, he recognized that he was not free to do whatever he pleased. He was under "the law of Christ" (1 Corinthians 9:21 NASB). We are to please others but not at the expense of God's standards (Galatians 1:10; 1 Thessalonians 2:4).

THE OBLIGATION OF GENEROSITY

In 2 Corinthians 8:7–9 the apostle Paul based his appeal for generosity on the example of Christ. "But just as you excel in everything— in faith, in speech, in knowledge, in complete earnestness and in your love for us—see that you also excel in this grace of giving," he wrote. "I am not commanding you, but I want to test the sincerity of your love by comparing it with the earnestness of others. For you know the grace of our Lord Jesus Christ, that though he was rich, yet for your sakes he became poor, so that you through his poverty might become rich."

Honoring God Through Our Wealth

The perception of some that the church is always asking for money has made it a taboo subject in many churches today. In an effort not to ruffle feathers, we have given the impression that God does not care what we do with our money. This is not true. According to Proverbs 3:9–10, one of the ways we honor the Lord is with our wealth. In the Old Testament, God's people were required to offer the "firstfruits"—they were to give the first part of their harvest as an offering to God. (For example, see Exodus 23:16, 19; 34:22; Deuteronomy 18:4; Nehemiah 10:35.)

The underlying principle behind this command was the message that God deserves first consideration in the believer's life and that He deserves the best part of whatever we offer to Him. The offering of the firstfruits was only a token that served to remind God's people that all they possessed came from Him. Old Testament scholar J. Barton Payne has noted: "Thus even when we yield up all that we have to God, the act constitutes but our expected service (Romans 6:12; 12:1); and it leaves us still as 'unprofitable servants' (Luke 17:10)."[8]

The New Testament does not tell believers to offer the firstfruits to God; instead it says that they *are* the firstfruits (James 1:18; cf. Revelation 14:4). They are themselves an offering to God. We are to offer ourselves first and then all that is ours.

Serving God . . . or Money

On one occasion Jesus praised a poor widow who had thrown two small coins into the temple treasury. This was far more impressive than the large amounts of money the rich had given, because they gave only out of their abundance. The widow, in contrast, had given all she had to live on (Mark 12:43–44). Money and our relationship to it is very much a matter of discipleship. Jesus warned that it is impossible to serve both God and money (Matthew 6:24; Luke 16:13).

In view of this, we should not view giving as an optional aspect of our worship. According to Jesus, the way we relate to our wealth and our possessions is a litmus test of our true devotion. It is an "either/or" proposition. Either we serve God or we serve money. Greed is itself a form of idolatry and is one of the things that sparks God's wrath (Colossians 3:5–6).

THREE CATEGORIES OF GIVING

The Old Testament Pattern

In Old Testament worship, the responsibility of giving fell into three broad categories. First was the obligation to give to God. Ultimately all offerings were given to the Lord. However, Israel's offerings were also used to support the priesthood. The priests and their families were permitted to eat some of the firstfruits the Israelites brought to the altar (Numbers 18:11–14). After the firstfruits, a tithe of what remained was also given to the Lord. This second kind of giving was used to support the Levites in their service (Leviticus 27:30–32). The Levites, in turn, gave a tenth of what they received to the priests. This was referred to as "the Lord's portion" (Numbers 18:26–28). Third, Israel's offerings were used to provide relief for the poor (Deuteronomy 14:28–29).

The New Testament Model

These same three categories are reflected in New Testament directives regarding giving. In Matthew 6:1–4 Jesus taught that giving should be done in secret so that God is the only audience. All that we give is given to God. Yet in this same passage what is offered to the Lord is also given to the needy. The importance of giving to the poor is a primary theme in other New Testament teaching about giving (Matthew 25:35–40; Luke 3:11; Romans 15:26; Galatians 2:10; James 1:27). Paul taught that the purpose of working is not merely to provide for one's own needs, but to have enough to give to the poor. "He who has been stealing must steal no longer, but must work, doing something useful with his own hands, that he may have something to share with those in need" (Ephesians 4:28).

The New Testament also emphasizes the church's obligation to use its finances to support the church's ministers. Paul often relied on the financial support of other churches to carry out his ministry (2 Corinthians 11:8–9; Philippians 4:18). He taught that those who are faithful in preaching and teaching should be paid for their services (1 Timothy 5:17–18). He even appealed to Old Testament precedent to provide a biblical rationale for this kind of giving. "Don't you know that those who work in the temple get their food from the temple, and those who serve at the altar share in what is offered on the altar? In the same way, the Lord has commanded that those who preach the gospel should receive their living from the gospel" (1 Corinthians 9:13–14; compare 1 Timothy 5:18). Giving is a matter of discipleship because those who give in a way that pleases God offer themselves to Him first (2 Corinthians 8:3–5).

An old proverb says that imitation is the sincerest form of flattery. But for the follower of Jesus it is a simple matter of obedience. The disciple's goal is to be like Christ the master. It is a goal made all the more certain by Christ's saving work. He is both the model and the means. The disciple's greatest hope is that when we see Him we shall be like Him.

SPIRITUAL FORMATION AND DISCIPLESHIP

THE DYNAMICS OF SPIRITUAL LIFE

Wendy was standing at a bus stop one morning when she noticed one of the other passengers staring at her. The two had waited at the same stop each day but had never spoken to one another. This morning Wendy smiled and struck up a conversation with him. They talked about various topics, and the stranger learned that Wendy was the registrar at a Christian seminary.

After a few minutes, the stranger asked her this odd question: "You're a holy woman, aren't you?"

Later, Wendy laughed and told me, "He knew that I worked at the seminary. I think he thought I was a nun."

When we talk about a life of discipleship, we are really talking about the spiritual life. The goal of the disciple is to be a "spiritual" person. But what does this really mean? For Wendy's acquaintance at the bus stop it was synonymous with a particular calling, like being a priest or nun. For others it is a feeling that is difficult to explain.

In today's world the notion of what it means to be a "spiritual" person is vague, even for many Christians. A surprising majority of Americans, for example, acknowledge that spirituality is an important part of their lives. A *Newsweek* poll a few years ago revealed that 58 percent of those who responded felt a need to experience spiritual growth. A slightly smaller but still surprisingly large 33 percent said that they have had a religious or mystical experience.

For many, however, their definition of what it means to be a spiritual person is like that of Rita McClain, a woman who was profiled in the same *Newsweek* article. McClain had been raised in a fundamentalist home but abandoned it at age twenty-seven for a religion of her own making. She had tried a universalist church, spent some time at a Buddhist meditation center, and studied Native American spiritual practices.

"These disparate rituals melded into a personal religion," *Newsweek* reported, "which McClain, a 50-year-old nurse, celebrates at an ever-changing altar in her home. Right now the altar consists of an angel statue, a small bottle of 'sacred water' blessed at a women's vigil, a crystal ball, a pyramid, a small brass leaf, a votive candle, a Hebrew prayer, a tiny Native American basket from the 1850s and a picture of her 'most sacred place,' a madrone tree near her home."[1]

Some professing Christians are not much clearer when it comes to the subject of spirituality. The Sunday school curriculum of one church in the Chicago area, for example, along with its study of the Bible, offers a course that promises to help those who attend understand the way God manifests His presence in dreams and the imagination. It also offers a course in ancient Chinese meditative practices, calling them "spiritual disciplines" that open one to religious experiences.

THE QUEST FOR SPIRITUALITY

It is no wonder we are confused. Spirituality seems to be the theme everywhere we look today. A championship professional basketball coach uses Buddhist principles to help him get the best out of his team. A best-selling author and motivational speaker draws on Eastern mysticism for the spiritual "laws" that lead to personal success. Another best-selling author uses the teachings of Jesus to help CEOs run their businesses. When we scan the television dial, we find popular shows that focus on the everyday adventures of angels, demons, vampires, ghosts, and at least one Protestant minister!

In the realm of science, recent research has identified the regions of the brain that are stimulated when someone has a religious experience, leading some scientists to conclude that spirituality is little more than a series of neurological changes in the brain's temporal lobes. Others argue that these perceived spiritual experiences are real and that the brain is merely recording them.[2]

Most people tend to define spirituality in personal rather than in biblical terms. We are not sure we can tell others what spirituality is, but we recognize it when we see it. This means that our notion of what it means to be spiritual is usually reduced to a mystical experience that is hard to describe and even harder to evaluate. Yet the Scriptures warn us that we have an obligation to test our "spiritual" experiences: "Do not believe every spirit, but test the spirits to see whether they are from God, because many false prophets have gone out into the world," writes the apostle John to the early church. Then he gives a test to help believers identify when the Spirit of God is in action: "Every spirit that acknowledges that Jesus Christ has come in the flesh is from God, but every spirit that does not acknowledge Jesus is not from God. This is the spirit of the antichrist, which you have heard is coming and even now is already in the world" (1 John 4:1–3).

The apostle's warning in these verses is based upon two important assumptions. The first assumption is that spiritual experiences are not self-validating. The mere fact that I have had a spiritual experience does not guarantee that God was the source. There are spirits that do not come from God and do not acknowledge Jesus Christ. A second important assumption is that it is possible to have a genuine spiritual experience that does not originate with God. Spiritual experiences must be tested by the truth of God's Word. We need to develop a theology of Christian spirituality.

What Does it Mean to Be Spiritual?

The obvious place to begin in understanding the nature of Christian spirituality is with that component of human nature known as "spirit." What is it? How did it originate and what happens to it during the process of regeneration and spiritual development?

Everyone Has a Spiritual Nature

Preacher and theologian James Boice has defined spirit as "that part of human nature that communes with God and partakes in some measure of God's own essence."[3] The origin of the human spirit is described in Genesis 2:7, which says that "the LORD God formed the man from the dust of the ground and breathed into his nostrils the breath of life, and the man became a living being." The spirit is what animates man and makes him "a living being."

It is significant that both the Hebrew and the Greek terms for spirit can also be translated "breath." The human spirit comes from the "breath" of God. Indeed, God is called "the Father of spirits" (Hebrews 12:9).

The New Testament speaks explicitly of the spiritual component of human nature when it asks: "For who among men knows the thoughts of a man except the man's spirit within him? In the same way no one knows the thoughts of God except the Spirit of God" (1 Corinthians 2:11). In this verse Paul points to the human spirit to help his readers understand the relationship between the Holy Spirit and the truths of Scripture. In the process, although it is not his primary intent, he also helps us to understand something about the human spirit. For example, he implies that every human being has a spiritual nature. The spirit is that part of us that dwells in our innermost thoughts. Paul also implies that the spirit is active even in those who are "spiritually dead." The implied answer to the question "Who among men knows the thoughts of a man except the man's spirit within him?" is "Nobody." Paul appeals to a universal experience to make his point.

Everybody has a functioning spirit in the sense spoken of in this verse. We might call this first level of spirituality a state of ordinary spirituality.

Our Spiritual Nature Is Damaged by Sin

The fact that everyone has a spiritual nature means that spirituality is not an exclusively Christian concept. One does not need to be a Christian to be interested in spirituality or even to have spiritual experiences. There is a fundamental problem, however, with non-Christian spirituality. Although every person has a spiritual nature, it is a nature that has been damaged by sin. Ephesians 2:1–3 characterizes our condition prior to trusting in Christ as a state of spiritual death: "As for you, you were dead in your transgressions and sins, in which you used to live when you followed the ways of this world and of the ruler of the kingdom of the air, the spirit who is now at work in those who are disobedient. All of us also lived among them at one time, gratifying the cravings of our sinful nature and following its desires and thoughts. Like the rest, we were by nature objects of wrath." Those who are spiritually dead are still spiritually active. They actively follow "the spirit now at work in those who are disobedient." They are controlled by the sinful nature and respond to its desires and thoughts.

To be spiritually dead is to be dead "in trespasses and sins." This spiritual condition originated with Adam, who was charged with the responsibility of caring for the Garden of Eden but was warned not to eat of the fruit of the Tree of the Knowledge of Good and Evil. He was told that when (literally "in the day") he ate of that tree he would "surely die" (Genesis 2:17). Adam disobeyed, was expelled from the Garden, had sons and daughters, and altogether lived for 930 years (Genesis 5:5). Yet spiritually speaking, Adam died the moment he ate of the forbidden tree. He proved this immediately after he disobeyed by fleeing from God's presence when he heard Him walking in the Garden (Genesis 3:8). He also proved it when, instead of taking responsibility for his sin, he shifted the blame to Eve (Genesis 3:12).

Adam's alienation from God was reflected in his veiled criticism of God when he was asked whether he had eaten from the forbidden tree: "The woman you put here with me—she gave me some fruit from the tree, and I ate it."

Adam's sin was bad enough. He had been created without a sin nature, had experienced intimate fellowship with God, and had been placed in a perfect environment. But the effects of his disobedience were so far reaching that we still suffer from them today. When Adam sinned, he did not sin for himself alone. He was serving as our representative. When he disobeyed, his sin was credited to our account, so that in God's eyes "all sinned" (Romans 5:12). In this way, Adam became the source of spiritual death for all humanity. From that moment, the human race began a downward spiral that removed the possibility of real communion with God and left us destructively self-centered. Adam's descendants did not lose interest in spiritual experiences or their capacity to worship. Instead, Romans 1:25 says: "They exchanged the truth of God for a lie, and worshiped and served created things rather than the Creator—who is forever praised. Amen."

We Suffer from "Total Depravity"

Religious practice continued after Adam sinned. The first murder ever committed was sparked by Cain's resentment when God accepted Abel's offering and rejected his (Genesis 4:3–8). But human nature was fundamentally altered. Theologians have used the phrase "total depravity" to describe human nature's fallen state.

The theologian Louis Berkhof clarified what is implied by this phrase, noting, "This does not mean that every man is as bad as he can be, cannot do good in any sense of the word, and has absolutely no sense of admiration for the true, the good, and the beautiful; but simply that the inherent corruption extends to every part of man's nature, and that there is in him no spiritual good, that is good in relation to God."[4]

CHRISTIAN SPIRITUALITY

Fortunately, God did not leave humanity in this helpless condition. Ephesians 2:4–7 describes His program of intervention: "But because of his great love for us, God, who is rich in mercy, made us alive with Christ even when we were dead in transgressions—it is by grace you have been saved. And God raised us up with Christ and seated us with him in the heavenly realms in Christ Jesus, in order that in the coming ages he might show the incomparable riches of his grace, expressed in his kindness to us in Christ Jesus." If ordinary spirituality is a state of spiritual death, the most important distinctive of Christian spirituality is that it is a state of spiritual life.

For the Christian, the conditions of spiritual alienation and condemnation described by Paul in Ephesians 2:1–3 are ancient history. Paul did not say that this is what Christians *are* but that it is what they once *were*. Something has changed for all those who are in Christ. They "have been made alive."

Further, Paul's language indicates that this new life is a particular kind of life. It is Christ's life. There are several dimensions to this experience of new life.

New Life Begins with the Forgiveness of Sin

Since spiritual death came as a result of sin, forgiveness is a precondition to spiritual life. Those who are spiritually dead are condemned by God's Law and enslaved by their own sinful nature. Christ's death wiped out the record of sin that made us God's enemies. This included the guilt of Adam's original sin that was credited to our account, along with all the interest we have compounded on that debt by our own sin.

The apostle Paul wrote that when God forgave us in Christ, He "cancelled out the certificate of debt consisting of decrees against us and which was hostile to us" (Colossians 2:14 NASB). In Paul's day, a "certificate of debt" was a legal record of what someone owed—equivalent to an IOU. Colossians 2:14 refers to the decrees of God's Law, obligations which were "hostile" or "against" us. Christ's sacrifice of Himself wiped away the debt we owed to God. Our debt was canceled when God "nailed it to the cross."

New Life Imparts a New Nature

Christ's death dealt with the penalty we were subject to because of sin. But the benefits of His work do not end there. Christ's resurrection dealt with the effects of sin. Christians have been "raised up" along with Christ. Paul's language in Ephesians 2:6 points to a reversal of the effects of Adam's sin in the believer's life. When we were spiritually dead, we lived in transgression and sin. Now that we have been raised with Christ we have the capacity to live a new life.

So while both the believer and the unbeliever have a spiritual nature, the believer's spiritual nature is significantly different from that of the unbeliever. The Christian's capacity to respond to God has been restored. This is the "new self" that believers are commanded to "put on" (Ephesians 4:24). Paul emphasized in Ephesians 4 that the new self has been "created to be like God in true righteousness and holiness" (v. 24). But in Colossians 3:10 he noted that this transformation is not an instantaneous one. This is because the new self is in the process of being "renewed in knowledge in the image of its Creator." This is not a contradiction. The gradual transformation described in Colossians 3:10 is the result of the new creation spoken of in Ephesians 4:24.

New Life Brings with It a New Position

After Christ rose from the dead, He ascended into heaven, where He is now seated at the right hand of the Father. (For example, see Acts 5:31; 7:55–56; Romans 8:34; Ephesians 1:20.) In biblical culture it was considered an honor to be seated at someone's right hand (1 Kings 2:19; Mark 10:37). This was a position of authority. Consequently, for Christ to be seated at the Father's right hand means that He is "far above all rule and authority, power and dominion, and every title that can be given, not only in the present age but also in the one to come" (Ephesians 1:21). His kingdom has not yet come in its fullness, but even now Christ reigns (1 Corinthians 15:24–25).

The fact that Christ is seated at the Father's right hand also means that His redemptive work is finished. He offered the one perfect sacrifice for all time. Nothing can be taken away from it, and nothing needs to be added to it. By this one sacrifice He made perfect those who are now going through the process of sanctification (Hebrews 10:12–13).

Yet if believers have died and risen with Christ, then it is also true that they have been exalted with Christ. Ephesians 2:6 says that we are now "seated . . . with [Christ] in the heavenly realms." Our physical location may be earthbound, but our position before God is one of being in Christ.

Christ's victory is our victory. All that Christ has purchased for us by His death, resurrection, and exaltation are already ours.

New Life Assures Us of a New Destiny

When we were apart from Christ, we were the objects of God's wrath. If it had not been for the intervention of God's grace, we would have been separated from Him for all eternity. Now that we have been seated in the heavenly realms in Christ we face a radically different future. God's purpose in raising us up with Christ and seating us with Him in the heavenly realms was "in order that in the coming ages he might show the incomparable riches of his grace, expressed in his kindness to us in Christ Jesus" (Ephesians 2:7).

What a destiny! We have exchanged an eternity of hopelessness and regret for an endless future of God's boundless kindness. This has not been our own doing. It is the work of God. It was His purpose from the very beginning (Ephesians 1:11–12). We who were once the objects of wrath have become heavenly trophies of grace.

THE ROLE OF THE HOLY SPIRIT

Before Spiritual Salvation: Conviction

One of the most important distinctives of Christian spirituality is the believer's unique relationship with the Holy Spirit. The Holy Spirit plays a central role both in our initial salvation experience and in the

Christian life that follows conversion. He is the special possession of everyone who knows Christ (Romans 8:9).

The Holy Spirit begins His work even before He comes to indwell us by convincing us of sin. When Jesus told the disciples that He would send the Holy Spirit, He promised that the Spirit would "convict the world of guilt in regard to sin and righteousness and judgment" (John 16:8). This is the language of the courtroom. To "convict" is to expose or bring to light. It is the Spirit's ministry to "the world," the work by which He makes sinners aware of their guilt, the nature of God's righteousness, and the inevitability of judgment.

During Salvation: Being Born Again

When we trust in Christ, the Holy Spirit imparts new life to us. Jesus referred to this as being "born again" (John 3:3, 8). The theological term for this work of the Holy Spirit is *regeneration.* It is mentioned in Titus 3:5, which says that God saved us: "by the washing of regeneration and renewing by the Holy Spirit" (NASB; see also KJV). Some New Testament scholars think that the language Paul used in this verse may have been part of an early Christian hymn that was sung as part of the baptismal service. Although it is possible that the "washing" and "renewing" mentioned in Titus 3:5 both refer to the same thing, it seems more likely that they speak of two distinct aspects of the believer's salvation experience. When we are born again, we are cleansed of sin ("washed"). Our guilt is taken away and we are given a new position as children of God.

At the same time, we are also given the capacity to live a new life ("renewing"). As a result of the work of Christ, the believer is made a "new creation" (2 Corinthians 5:17; Galatians 6:15). "No one has understood the gospel" John Stott asserts, "who has not grasped that Christianity is first inward and spiritual, and secondly a divine work of grace."[5]

Upon Salvation: A Deposit of What's to Come

The presence of the Holy Spirit marks the believer as God's own child. He is described as a "seal" in Ephesians 1:13. In the ancient world seals were often placed on documents to identify ownership and guarantee authenticity. We are sealed with the Holy Spirit when we believe, and His presence guarantees God's blessings to us until we receive the promised inheritance.

He is also called a "deposit" (2 Corinthians 1:22; Ephesians 1:14). The word used in these two verses was used in other Greek writings to refer to the down payment or "earnest" paid on a piece of property. When my wife and I bought our home, the real estate agent asked us to pay a certain amount of money before the deal was finalized to prove that we were willing to follow through with the purchase. He referred to this payment as "earnest money." When Paul speaks of the Holy Spirit as the earnest that guarantees what is to come, he implies that part of the Holy Spirit's ministry is to give us a foretaste of what our final experience of salvation will be like. It might be said that the Holy Spirit enables the believer to experience a little bit of heaven on earth!

More than that, the Holy Spirit's presence assures us that salvation will be a certainty. As Charles Ryrie explained, "The fact that God gives the earnest of the Spirit binds Him to fully complete the salvation He has begun in the believer."[6]

Upon Salvation: Assurance We Are God's Children

Assurance of salvation is one of the ministries of the Holy Spirit. He "testifies with our spirit that we are God's children" (Romans 8:16). Doubts may still arise, but it is the Spirit that quiets them. The Holy Spirit is also called "the Spirit of sonship" (Romans 8:15), or "the spirit of adoption" (NASB). It is the Holy Spirit who prompts us to address God as a child would a father. He mediates our experience of God's love by "pouring" it into our hearts (Romans 5:5).

The Holy Spirit's ministry is a source of power for the Christian, but it is a mistake to think of Him as an impersonal force. He is a Person, not a power. Because He is a personal Being, He spoke to the New Testament church, and He prays for us when we don't know how to pray (Acts 13:2; Romans 8:26). Because the Holy Spirit is a Person, He can be grieved by us (Ephesians 4:30). We grieve God's Spirit when we engage in unwholesome speech and when we allow bitterness and anger to divide the body of Christ (Ephesians 4:29, 31).

THE EVIDENCE OF THE SPIRIT

Spiritual Gifts

One of the Holy Spirit's most important ministries is to equip the church for service. He is the source of spiritual gifts. Sadly, this has been the subject of considerable confusion and division within the church. Some Christians claim that all the gifts described in the New Testament are still functioning today. Others believe that only certain gifts are to be expected in the current age. Both views have certain strengths, and both have inherent dangers. As we look at each position, let's remember the purpose of spiritual gifts: They are given to unify and strengthen the church; they should not create divisions.

Those who claim that all the spiritual gifts should still be the norm in the church today rightly point out that there is no explicit statement in the New Testament indicating that sign gifts like tongues, miracles, and healing were expected to cease at the end of the apostolic age. The assertion of 1 Corinthians 13:8–10 that tongues and prophecy would cease "when perfection comes" hardly qualifies. It establishes only that these gifts serve a temporary purpose in the life of the church and that they will no longer be necessary when the church reaches a state of full maturity. It is significant, however, that Acts 2:43 says that miraculous signs were performed by the apostles. This agrees with the apostle Paul's characterization of signs, wonders, and miracles as "the things that mark an apostle" (2 Corinthians 12:12; cf. Hebrews 2:3–4). This suggests that these gifts served a foundational purpose. They confirmed the ministry of the apostles whose function was to establish the church (Ephesians 2:20).

On the other hand, those of us who believe that the miraculous gifts ceased at the end of the apostolic era often find ourselves in the unenviable position of defining our theology of the Holy Spirit primarily in terms of what we believe God will *not* do. We are quick to explain away reports of the miraculous among believers today, at times attributing such things to Satan. The Scriptures do teach that Satan is able to empower his servants to perform counterfeit miracles and that such things will be a feature of the coming of the Antichrist (2 Thessalonians 2:9). Yet we ought to be very careful about setting God's agenda for Him. Daniel B. Wallace, a professor of New Testament studies at Dallas Theological Seminary, has rightly observed, "Although the sign gifts died in the first century, the Holy Spirit did not. We can affirm this theologically, but pragmatically we act as though the Holy Spirit died with the early church."[7]

Can God still perform miraculous works through the church? Undoubtedly, He can. His power has not diminished. Would He use signs, wonders, and miracles today? That is a more difficult question. In view of the place these works had in the early church, it would seem best to conclude that if they do happen today, they are unusual occurrences. We should not expect them to be normative in the life of the believer. However, perhaps the greatest problem, both for the charismatic believer (who holds all gifts are still in effect) and the noncharismatic believer alike, is that we tend to be more interested in the gifts than we are in the God who is their author.

This misplaced focus leads to presumption. Wallace has warned, "The problem with some charismatics is that they believe that God not only can heal, but that he must heal. God thus becomes an instrument, wielded by the almighty Christian. At the same time, the problem with noncharismatics is that although we claim that God can heal, we act as if he won't."[8] The Holy Spirit is not at our beck and call. He distributes gifts throughout the body of Christ according to His sovereign will. Every believer is given the Holy Spirit and is gifted in some way, but not everyone has the same gifts (1 Corinthians 12:29–30).

We are told to desire the greater gifts, but we are also reminded that we cannot control which ones will be given to us. "All these are the work of one and the same Spirit," the apostle Paul declares, "and he gives them to each one, just as he determines" (1 Corinthians 12:11). The tension between the assertions of these passages is deliberate. According to New Testament scholar D. A. Carson, "Paul's aim is not to discourage Christians from pursuing what is best, but to prevent them from making any one gift the sine qua non, the sign without which one might legitimately call into question whether the Holy Spirit was present and active."9

The Fruit of the Spirit

Ironically, the church's ongoing dispute over spiritual gifts has obscured what really should be regarded as the primary evidence for the presence of the Holy Spirit in the believer's life. The Holy Spirit's presence is most often seen, not in gifts of the Spirit but in the fruit of the Spirit (Galatians 5:22–23). Qualities like love, joy, peace, patience, kindness, goodness, faithfulness, gentleness, and self-control are the everyday miracles that prove to the world that Christ has done a transforming work in the believer's life. They are the marks of true spirituality among believers.

Spiritual gifts are important to the life of the church, but they do not guarantee spiritual maturity. The church of Corinth was one of the most gifted churches in the New Testament. Yet it was this same church that the apostle Paul described as "worldly" and as "mere infants in Christ" (1 Corinthians 3:1). Galatians 6:1 commands that those who are "spiritual" are to restore other believers who are caught in a sin. It is no accident that this command follows Paul's list of the fruit of the Spirit in Galatians 5:22–23. Paul's command also implies a distinction between believers. Apparently, not everyone is automatically fitted for this task of restoring those who are overtaken by sin. It is a responsibility laid upon those Paul categorizes as spiritual—those who are "in step" with the Holy Spirit and whose lives are marked by His fruit (Galatians 5:25).

SPIRITUALITY TODAY

In view of this, the Scriptures seem to indicate that there are actually three levels of spirituality. The lowest level is what we might call universal spirituality. Every human being has a spiritual nature

(1 Corinthians 2:11). The second level might be described as Christian spirituality. Believers are spiritual in a way that ordinary people are not, because Christians are indwelt by the Holy Spirit. This is the condition of every believer (Romans 8:9). However, the command of Galatians 6:1 adds a third category when it categorizes some believers as "spiritual," implying that others are not. "Spiritual" in this sense must mean spiritually mature.

Today's renewed interest in spiritual matters is probably a good thing. It provides us with many opportunities to talk about Christ's work. But the church should not confuse the world's definition of spirituality with the spirituality of the Bible. Christian spirituality is unique. In God's eyes, it is the only true spirituality.

In the end, Wendy's acquaintance at the bus stop was right. She was a "holy woman." Not because of her vocation but because of Jesus Christ had done for her. His death and resurrection had given her a new status before God, a new nature, and had enabled her to enter into a new relationship with the Holy Spirit, whose transforming work was evident in her life.

OBSTACLES
TO DISCIPLESHIP

WHY SOME
FAIL TO GROW

When our children took their first steps, my wife and I could not have been happier if they had sat down at the piano and played a Beethoven sonata. Jane noted the event in a special journal that marked each child's major developmental milestones of their early years. Each journal celebrated the first step, the first word, their first tooth, and highlighted the day they got on the bus to attend their first day of school.

Like most parents, we felt a little anxious when others their age showed signs of growth ahead of schedule and eagerly waited until our children caught up with their friends. However, while we were proud of each new accomplishment, we were not surprised. We expected our children to grow and develop. In the natural realm, growth is normal.

The same is true in the spiritual realm. Normally, spiritual birth should lead to spiritual growth and development. Yet this is not always the case. Some who have professed faith in Jesus Christ appear to suffer from "stunted" growth. Years after their conversion they are still much the same as when they first believed. This is not a new problem. New Testament Christians struggled with it as well. The author of the book of Hebrews complained that at the time when his readers ought to have been able to teach others, they needed to be taught the "elementary truths of God's word all over again" (Hebrews 5:12). The writer's complaint sheds light both on the dynamics of spiritual growth and on some of the factors that contribute to spiritual immaturity.

PROGRESSIVE GROWTH

One of the assumptions behind the complaint of Hebrews 5:12 is the expectation that normal Christian growth should occur over time: "By this time you ought to be teachers." This statement indicates that it is reasonable to expect a certain measure of growth to take place once we have trusted in Christ. At the same time, it implies that this growth experience is progressive in nature. Spiritual maturity is not attained instantaneously when we experience the new birth. The earliest stage of the believer's spiritual development might be described as a state of normal immaturity.

When an infant comes home from the hospital and begins to cry for its dinner, its parents are not going to make it a peanut butter sandwich or broil it a steak. A hungry infant will be fed on milk or formula because its digestive system is not ready for solid food. When the same child is a little older it will be ready for solid food, but even then its meals will not be as substantial as those it will enjoy later on.

According to the author of Hebrews, those who are in a state of spiritual infancy need "spiritual milk," while those who are spiritually mature require the biblical equivalent to "solid food." "Anyone who lives on milk," he explains, "being still an infant, is not acquainted with the teaching about righteousness. But solid food is for the mature, who by constant use have trained themselves to distinguish good from evil" (Hebrews 5:13–14). During the stage of spiritual infancy, the new Christian's capacity to understand biblical truth is limited in much the same way that an infant is limited in his or her capacity to digest certain foods. The proper focus during this stage of development is upon the first principles of the Christian faith.

We get an idea of what some of these first principles are from Hebrews 6:1–2. They include teaching about the need to reject sin and turn to God in faith. The writer's list of fundamentals also includes an emphasis upon the inevitability of resurrection and impending judgment. In addition to these subjects, the writer of Hebrews addresses topics especially suited to the Jewish context of his readers when he mentions teaching about "baptisms and laying on of hands." The term "baptisms" in Hebrews 6:2 probably did not refer to the practice of Christian baptism. It is more likely that the author used it to speak of the kind of ritual washing that was common in New Testament Judaism.

The practice of laying hands on someone was common both in New Testament Judaism and in Christianity. In Judaism, it was symbolic of consecration or commissioning (Numbers 27:18–19; Deuteronomy 34:9). It was also a symbol of substitution. During the sacrificial ceremony, the Israelite worshiper placed his hand upon the offering to signify that its blood was being offered in his place. (For example, see Leviticus 1:4; 3:2; 4:4.)

In the New Testament church, the laying on of hands symbolized the bestowal of the Holy Spirit and His gifts. The apostle Paul urged Timothy to "fan into flame the gift of God, which is in you through the laying on of my hands" (2 Timothy 1:6; compare with 1 Timothy 4:14; Acts 8:18–19). The early church also placed their hands on those who were being commissioned for special service (Acts 6:6; 13:3). In the case of these Hebrew Christians, instruction about the first principles of the faith included teaching that was meant to help them see the difference between the gospel of grace and the works-oriented legalism of their Jewish heritage.

STAGES OF GROWTH

From Infancy . . . to Adolescence . . . to Maturity

Spiritual growth, like human growth, develops in stages. John mentions three stages (in inverted chronological order) in 1 John 2:13

(and repeats in part in v. 14): "I write to you, fathers, because you have known him who is from the beginning. I write to you, young men, because you have overcome the evil one. I write to you, dear children, because you have known the Father." Perhaps we could label these stages spiritual infancy, adolescence, and maturity.

John does not explain in detail how each stage differs from the others. He does, however, provide us with some basic clues. According to John, spiritual infancy and spiritual maturity are both characterized by the knowledge of God. This is not surprising. Jesus taught His disciples that the knowledge of God is the essence of eternal life: "Now this is eternal life: that they may know you, the only true God, and Jesus Christ, whom you have sent" (John 17:3). Knowing God is both the beginning and end of the Christian life. Knowledge, as it is used in these verses, does not refer primarily to a cognitive awareness of biblical doctrine but to a growing relationship.

Such a relationship begins with the knowledge of what God the Father has done for us through the person of Jesus Christ. Jesus is "the radiance of God's glory and the exact representation of his being" (Hebrews 1:3). This means that the more we know about Jesus Christ, the more we know about God the Father. Jesus reveals the Father and gives us access to a relationship with Him when we place our trust in Jesus (John 14:6–7). This relationship is deepened as our knowledge and experience of God grow. The spiritual infant knows God by faith. The spiritually mature believer knows Him by faith and experience.

The Ongoing Struggle

The distinguishing mark of spiritual adolescence according to 1 John 2:13–14 is victory over the Evil One. We can conclude from this that normal spiritual development is characterized by growth in obedience as well as growth in knowledge. The believer's skill in saying no to sin and yes to God increases as he or she progresses in the Christian life. This does not necessarily mean that our struggle with the flesh diminishes as we mature. In some cases it may even grow more intense. This is because understanding of sin deepens as we mature, to the point where it not only includes our actions but also the motives that prompt them.

One obvious implication of this is that not every Christian is in the same place spiritually. Spiritual growth is progressive. It moves from infancy to adulthood. We shouldn't be too surprised, then, to find a range of spiritual levels in the church. The church's strategy for discipleship must take this into account by providing a range of opportunities for believers at every level of development. This is also good to know if I am at an early stage in my spiritual development.

Perhaps you are someone who has just recently trusted in Christ and is feeling a little frustrated. It may seem to you as if everyone else is confident and self-assured in their Christian experience. You have thousands of questions about your faith, and others do not appear to have any. You struggle with the changes you need to make in your life, and they do not appear to share your struggle. Some of the things that you read in Scripture seem so lofty that you fear you will never understand them. If this sounds like your situation, don't become discouraged. In time you will grow. It is very likely that you have already grown more than you realize.

STUNTED GROWTH

Should we assume, however, that spiritual growth just "happens" in the Christian life? Is our part merely to wait long enough for growth to occur? Or do we have a greater responsibility? Those who received the letter to the Hebrews had been Christians long enough for the writer to expect them to have grown to a level of spiritual maturity. Instead, they had remained spiritual infants. The reason for this was because they had been "slow to learn" (Hebrews 5:11). The Greek adjective translated "slow" in this verse is a term that was commonly used in the New Testament era to speak of sluggishness or neglect. They had grown sluggish in their understanding of God's truth and had become slothful in applying it to their lives.

As a result, they had stalled in their spiritual development. That had not always been the case. Hebrews 10:32–34 indicates that these same believers had begun their Christian experiences with considerable enthusiasm, even to the point where they had been willing to joyfully accept the confiscation of their property because of their personal commitment to Jesus Christ.

The apostle Paul expressed a complaint similar to that of the author of Hebrews in 1 Corinthians 3. "Brothers, I could not address you as spiritual but as worldly—mere infants in Christ. I gave you milk, not solid food, for you were not yet ready for it. Indeed, you are still not ready" (v. 1–2). The tone of this statement is one of surprise. Paul had expected the Corinthians to be "spiritual." Instead, he found that they were "worldly," or as the Greek text literally says, "fleshly."

To understand the implications of this statement, it is helpful to compare it with similar language used by Paul earlier in the letter. In 1 Corinthians 2, Paul contrasted the "natural" man with the "spiritual" man (vv. 14–15 NASB) and said: "The man without the Spirit does not accept the things that come from the Spirit of God, for they are foolishness to him, and he cannot understand them, because they are spiritually discerned" (v. 14 NIV). Although Paul spoke of an inability to accept spiritual truth in both cases, there is an important but subtle difference between them. The person described in 1 Corinthians 2:14 is one who is devoid of the Holy Spirit. In the Greek text he is characterized as a "soulish" man. The "soulish" man cannot accept the things that come from God's Spirit (i.e., the truths Paul was teaching) because they are "spiritually discerned." He lacks the spiritual capacity to see their value and is unresponsive to God's truth. Because he is spiritually dead, he is incapable of opening his heart to it.

The same cannot be said of the "spiritual infant" described in 1 Corinthians 3:1. This person is "spiritual" in the sense that he possesses the Holy Spirit. But he is not spiritually mature. He is "worldly." In 1 Corinthians 2:14–15 Paul explained that the natural or "soulish" man cannot do what the "spiritual" man can do. But in 1 Corinthians 3:1 he wrote that he could not address the Corinthians as "spiritual." This was a stinging rebuke. In effect, Paul was telling this church, one which prided itself in its great teaching and its wisdom, that its spiritual capacity was on a par with an unbeliever. This condition forced Paul to adjust his teaching to suit the Corinthians' spiritual state. He treated them like spiritual babies and gave them "milk" instead of "solid food" (1 Corinthians 3:2).

It is sobering to consider that the Corinthians probably did not see themselves as Paul did. They saw themselves as spiritual and mature, when in reality they were fleshly and immature. The proof of their immaturity was seen in the presence of jealousy and quarreling within the church. "You are still worldly," Paul wrote. "For since there is jealousy and quarreling among you, are you not worldly? Are you not acting like mere men?" (1 Corinthians 3:3).

We tend to think of spiritual maturity in terms of what a person knows. If someone discusses difficult doctrines, reads complex theological works, or listens to the most capable Bible teachers, then we say that he or she is mature. Paul's rebuke indicates that God uses a different standard to measure spiritual maturity. The mark of spiritual maturity is not merely the possession of knowledge. True maturity is characterized by applied knowledge. Jesus Himself emphasized this when He said: "If you hold to my teaching, you are really my disciples" (John 8:31).

Am I spiritually mature? That depends. It does not depend only on what I know, but also upon how I respond to what I know. The believer whose life is dominated by the things that the Bible characterizes as the works of the flesh is spiritually immature, no matter how much content he or she may have mastered.

GROWTH STOPPERS

A "Fleshly" (Sinful) Nature

The primary hindrance to spiritual growth, then, is this aspect of our nature that the Bible refers to as the "flesh." Most of us use the word *flesh* to speak of our skin. Although the Bible also uses it in this sense, often the New Testament term for "flesh" refers to that part of our nature that is bent on resisting God. It is that dimension of our nature that continues to reflect disfigurement of sin. The flesh is actually the "sinful nature."

According to Romans 7:5, every time God's Law comes into contact with the sinful nature, it stirs up sinful passions deep within us. Because of this, those who only have the sinful nature are incapable of pleasing God, despite their good intentions (Romans 8:8).

Prior to our trusting in Jesus Christ as Savior, the sinful nature was the only nature we had. Once we placed our faith in Christ, an important change took place. We received spiritual life and were indwelt by the Holy Spirit. The presence of the Holy Spirit meant that we no longer had to be controlled by the sinful nature. "You, however, are controlled not by the sinful nature but by the Spirit, if the Spirit of God lives in you. And if anyone does not have the Spirit of Christ, he does not belong to Christ. But if Christ is in you, your body is dead because of sin, yet your spirit is alive because of righteousness" (Romans 8:9–10).

It is important to note that the Holy Spirit does not eradicate the sinful nature in the believer. The flesh is still present and continues to exert an influence in the believer's life. Its continuing presence often leads to struggle: "For the sinful nature ("flesh" NASB) desires what is contrary to the Spirit, and the Spirit what is contrary to the sinful nature. They are in conflict with each other, so that you do not do what you want" (Galatians 5:17).

The presence of the flesh is one of the main deterrents to spiritual growth in the Christian life. Whenever I allow myself to be controlled by the sinful nature, my attitudes and actions are the opposite of what God intends. As long as I live according to the flesh, I will become more like the sinful nature and less like Jesus Christ. This means that I may be my own worst enemy in the spiritual life. This is what the Puritan theologian John Owen meant when he warned: "Your enemy is not only upon you, as on Samson of old, but is in you also."[1]

A "Worldly" Christian

The result of living in the flesh is something that Paul has described as "worldliness." This was the problem of the Corinthian church. We sometimes use the term "worldly" to refer to those who engage in practices like smoking, drinking, dancing, or any other activity that we might deem unsuitable for the Christian. These things may indeed be "worldly," but the apostle Paul's list of worldly behavior in 1 Corinthians 3:3 focuses on internal attitudes like jealousy and more "acceptable" sins (to many Christians) like quarreling: "For since there is jealousy and quarreling among you, are you not worldly? Are you not acting like mere men?"

According to Paul, a worldly Christian is one who acts like a "mere man." This criticism implies that those who belong to Christ are more than "merely" human. There is a divine dimension to their behavior. They are "partakers of the divine nature" through the promises of God's Word and the empowerment of the Holy Spirit (2 Peter 1:4).

GROWTH AND EFFORT

The Source of Growth: God Himself

Although spiritual growth is ultimately a matter of grace, it requires a measure of Spirit empowered effort to take place. The author of Hebrews linked spiritual growth to growth in obedience when he wrote, "Solid food is for the mature, who by constant use have trained themselves to distinguish good from evil" (Hebrews 5:14). We do not become spiritually mature simply because we acquire doctrinal and biblical knowledge. Truth is a necessary catalyst for spiritual growth, but true growth occurs only when truth is applied. At every stage in our development we are responsible to add to the knowledge and virtues that we have already attained in Christ.

God's grace and power have provided all that "we need for life and godliness," the apostle Peter wrote. Indeed, God has "given us his very great and precious promises, so that through them [we] may participate in the divine nature and escape the corruption in the world caused by evil desires" (2 Peter 1:3–4).

"For this very reason," Peter continued, "make every effort to add to your faith goodness; and to goodness, knowledge; and to knowledge, self-control; and to self-control, perseverance; and to perseverance, godliness; and to godliness, brotherly kindness; and to brotherly kindness, love" (vv. 5–7).

Notice that spiritual development begins with faith. This faith serves as the foundation for adding all the virtues that are characteristic of a fully mature believer. Our confidence in God's power and promises motivate us to make the necessary effort to add these virtues to our faith.

Our obligation in the process of spiritual growth is to be responsive to the power of God that is itself the ultimate cause of growth. This important spiritual dynamic is indicated by the author of Hebrews, who used a passive form of the verb to urge his readers to "go on to maturity" in Hebrews 6:1. New Testament scholar Donald Guthrie noted, "This form suggests an element of yieldedness to a nobler influence, as if the maturing process is not a matter of our ingenuity. Spiritual maturity is not the kind which can be had for the asking, but requires higher powers than man's natural endowments."[2]

Our "Making Every Effort" Brings Assurance and Maturity

The importance of "making every effort" to mature in the Christian life is further underscored by the connection Peter makes between the presence of these virtues in the believer and the experience of assurance. One of the dangers of being in a persistent state of immaturity is that it may cause us to question the reality of our salvation. It is clear from Peter's words that some who lack the characteristics he describes are truly born again. They are merely suffering from a problem of spiritual vision. He explains that those who possess these qualities in an increasing measure ensure that that they will be effective and productive in their knowledge of Jesus Christ (2 Peter 1:8). But, he warns, the one who does not possess them is "nearsighted" and "blind" and has "forgotten that he has been cleansed from his past sins" (2 Peter 1:9).

In view of this, Peter urges his readers, "Therefore, my brothers, be all the more eager to make your calling and election sure. For if you do these things, you will never fall, and you will receive a rich welcome into the eternal kingdom of our Lord and Savior Jesus Christ" (2 Peter 1:10–11). This is the language of commerce. To make something sure in this sense is to guarantee it.

One of the most sobering implications of these two verses is the possibility that some may never go on to spiritual maturity because they are not among those whose calling and election are guaranteed. In other words, they do not grow because they do not really belong to Christ. They are Christians by profession only and have not truly experienced the grace of God that leads to spiritual growth.

The author of the book of Hebrews seems to hold a similar view of the relationship between maturity and assurance. After urging his readers to go on to spiritual maturity, the writer warns, "It is impossible for those who have once been enlightened, who have tasted the heavenly gift, who have shared in the Holy Spirit, who have tasted the goodness of the word of God and the powers of the coming age, if they fall away, to be brought back to repentance, because to their loss they are crucifying the Son of God all over again and subjecting him to public disgrace" (Hebrews 6:4–6).

Despite the difficulties in this passage, several things are clear about those described in it. They clearly have had more than a passing knowledge of the gospel and its claims. They have been "enlightened" in some way and have experienced the ministry of the Holy Spirit in a powerful way. Despite these advantages, they have renounced Jesus Christ and His work in a most decisive way. This is not the same thing as "lapsing" or "backsliding." Those described in Hebrews 6:4–6 regard Jesus Christ with such contempt that it is as if they crucify Him all over again (cf. Hebrews 10:29). The analogy that follows compares their behavior to land that is unable to produce a crop and "is in danger of being cursed" (Hebrews 6:8). Their defection from the faith is evidence of their true spiritual state.

The Ingredients for Growth

Fundamentally, spiritual growth comes from God. The Corinthians made the mistake of thinking that the secret to growth was to be found in the personality of the one doing the teaching. They had divided into factions over their favorite Bible teachers (1 Corinthians 1:12; 3:4). Paul redirected their focus to the power of God that made their favorite teachers effective. People like Paul and Apollos had indeed been used by God in a remarkable way, but in the end they were only servants who had been assigned a task to fulfill. In the end, God's power was the only thing that mattered (1 Corinthians 3:5–7).

We must avoid two opposite but equally dangerous extremes. One extreme is the trap that the Corinthian church fell into. It is possible to exalt the means used by God to foster spiritual growth beyond measure. The mistake the Corinthians made was to look to men when they should have been looking to God. They had attributed the church's growth to their favorite teachers and vicariously took credit for it themselves because of their association with them. They foolishly acted as if these teachers were in competition with one another.

The other extreme that must be avoided is to ignore the means that God has provided for spiritual growth. On the surface it might seem as if Paul's words to the Corinthians rule out the need for human teachers. The one who sows and the one who reaps are "nothing," Paul wrote; it is God who causes growth (1 Corinthians 3:6–7). Yet at the same time Paul clearly indicated that the God who gave growth also chose to use human instruments in this process. God could have chosen to bring people to new life in Christ without human instrumentality, but instead He entrusted the gospel to the church and commanded that it be preached throughout the whole world (Matthew 24:14; 28:18–20). He could also have made it so that the new believer would instantaneously grow from spiritual infancy to maturity in a moment. Instead, He ordained that spiritual development take place over time and be linked to certain means that foster growth.

Consequently, while the teacher is "nothing," we can also be fairly sure that the one who has never been exposed to teaching will remain spiritually immature. First John 2:27 notes that the Holy Spirit carries on an internal ministry of teaching so that "you do not need anyone to teach you." Yet Ephesians 4:11–12 indicates that the same God who gave the Holy Spirit also gave the church "pastors and teachers to prepare God's people for works of service, so that the body of Christ may be built up."

FOUNDATIONAL TOOLS

The Word of God

If spiritual maturity requires a measure of Spirit empowered human effort, what are the tools used by the Spirit to foster spiritual growth? First and foremost is the Word of God. When it comes to natural growth, diet plays a crucial role in promoting healthy development. Diet also plays an important part in spiritual growth. In 1 Peter 2:2–3 the apostle urges his readers to "crave pure spiritual milk, so that by it you may grow up in your salvation, now that you have tasted that the Lord is good." We are not merely to dabble in it. According to 1 Peter 2:2 it is not enough merely to read it or even study it. We are to "crave" it. This is the language of intense longing. The same Hebrew word was used by the apostle Paul to speak of the longing one person feels for another (Romans 1:11; Philippians 1:8; 2:26; 1 Thessalonians 3:6; 2 Timothy 1:4). He also used it to describe the believer's intense desire to be clothed with the resurrection body (2 Corinthians 5:2).

Those who grow spiritually do not merely enjoy the Scriptures; they have a desire for it that is equal to the most fundamental longings of human experience. Their longing to know God by His Word is as intense as Job's when he said: "I have not departed from the commands of his lips; I have treasured the words of his mouth more than my daily bread" (Job 23:12).

This poses an interesting dilemma. How can we create within ourselves a longing for God's Word that is so strong that we desire it the way a thirsty man longs for water? For example, I have never liked asparagus. I might choose to eat it on the grounds that it is good for me, but I doubt that I will ever really enjoy it. No matter how much I "will" myself to like it, I will never "long" for it. Is Peter saying that the Scriptures are different? Can we create a hunger for God's Word by the sheer force of our will?

The secret to understanding Peter's statement lies in his carefully chosen analogy. He does not compare God's Word to an "acquired" taste like vegetables but to milk, something that infants naturally crave. He also links the longing he asks us to have to personal experience. After commanding his readers to long for God's Word, he qualifies it with this all-important condition in 1 Peter 2:3: "now that you have tasted that the Lord is good." How do we develop the craving for a particular food in the natural realm? We taste it and find that we like it. This same principle operates in the spiritual realm. The best way to develop a hunger for God's Word is to "taste that the Lord is good."

Prayer

Prayer is another of the foundational tools God uses to foster spiritual growth. Prayer works together with the Scriptures to transform the believer's life and thinking. Paul prayed for the Colossians that God would fill them with "the knowledge of his will through all spiritual wisdom and understanding" (Colossians 1:9). In his epistle James promises that everyone who asks God for wisdom in genuine faith would receive it (James 1:5).

Prayer can also affect our behavior. When Paul asked God to help the Colossians understand the Scriptures, he also asked Him to enable them to "live a life worthy of the Lord and . . . please him in every way" (Colossians 1:10). An old saying reminds us that "prayer changes things." It might be added that prayer also changes people.

R. A. Torrey underscored the foundational role of prayer in the disciple's spiritual life when he noted: "Other things being equal, your growth and mine will be in exact proportion to the time and to the heart we put into prayer."[3] In saying this, Torrey emphasized that the heart is as important as time in this equation. "I put it in this way because there are many who put a great deal of time into praying," Torrey explained, "but they put so little heart into their praying that they do very little praying in the long time they spend at it; while there are others who perhaps may not put so much time into praying but who put as much heart into their praying, that they accomplish vastly more by their praying in a short time than the others accomplish by praying in a long time."4

The Norm

My children have yet to play a Beethoven sonata. But they did learn to play the piano. This skill did not come automatically. It required a combination of natural development, specialized training, and daily practice. When they stopped taking piano lessons several years ago, they also quit practicing. At that point, their development in this area came to a halt. Indeed, if they were to sit down at the piano today, they would find it extremely difficult, if not impossible, to perform music that they had once played well. This is similar to the Christian life. Spiritual growth is expected but does not come without a combination of training and practice.

God is the ultimate source of all spiritual development, but He has chosen to use means to promote it. Chief among them are prayer and the Scriptures. Those who neglect the appointed means of growth and fail to practice Christian virtues will see their spiritual life decline. Graces previously acquired may disappear. They may even begin to question whether there was ever a genuine transformation in their lives in the first place. When they ought to be mature enough to teach others, they will need to go back to kindergarten and learn the first principles of the Christian life all over again.

Got milk?

THE MACHINERY
OF HOLINESS

THE ROLE OF THE
BODY IN DISCIPLESHIP

How important is the body? Very important, judging from a quick scan of the magazine rack at the checkout counter of the local grocery store. Although the news tabloids for sale there focus on a wide and often bizarre assortment of issues, ranging from space aliens masquerading as government officials to the latest breakup in Hollywood, three subjects will always reappear in the headlines: our diet, our health, and our appearance.

Judging from the tabloid headlines, ranging from "Lose 10 Pounds in Five Days!" to "Try Our Miracle Makeover," most people's interest in the body seems to be primarily ornamental. Yes, we value the benefits of good health, but mostly we long for rock-hard "abs," thin thighs, or whatever else will help us to feel like we resemble the "beautiful people" whose pictures grace the cover of these same tabloids and magazines. The primary function of the body, it would seem, is to be put on display.

This is not a purely secular phenomenon. Some of these same themes have also been reflected in Christian publishing. Ruth Marie Griffith, for example, has traced the explosion of interest in Christian diet literature in the United States from the 1950s through the 1990s and has noticed some similarities with secular organizations like Overeaters Anonymous and Weight Watchers. While methods and language may seem similar, there is one fundamental difference between these "Christian" programs and their secular counterparts. Evangelical writers are not merely interested in the body for cosmetic reasons. Their interest is ultimately a spiritual one.

Griffith explains, "The body is God's temple, these writers remind their readers, and the real aim of keeping it 'under subjection'—thin, firm, disciplined—is not mere self-gratification but sacrificial obedience to God."[1]

THE BIBLICAL VIEW OF THE BODY

The Body Versus the Spirit

But does the body have anything to do with the life of the spirit? Why is the body important? What is God's purpose for the body, both now and in eternity? In one sense, life in the body might be seen as the antithesis to the life of the spirit, if not an outright obstacle. Reformation theologian John Calvin referred to the body as the "prison house" of the soul. In his view the soul was the more noble part of man.[2]

In saying this, Calvin agreed with the conviction of earlier theologians. Augustine regarded the body as the lowest part of man.[3] It is easy to see why. The Scriptures sometimes refer to the body in a way that seems to cast it in a negative light. Using the analogy of an athlete in training, Paul said that he "beat" his body in order to make it his "slave" (1 Corinthians 9:27). He also said that he was a prisoner of the law of sin at work in the "members" of his body (Romans 7:23). He concluded his discussion of indwelling sin with the anguished cry: "What a wretched man I am! Who will rescue me from this body of death?" (Romans 7:24).

The apparent dichotomy between body and spirit that Augustine and Calvin both noted was reflected in Paul's observation about God's Law: "We know that the law is spiritual; but I am unspiritual, sold as a slave to sin" (Romans 7:14).

Sin's Effect Upon the Body: Degradation and Decay

However, when Paul said that he was "unspiritual," he did not mean that there was a fundamental disparity between God's Law and the body. The root problem for Paul was not that he had a body but the effect that sin had upon his body. This effect was something that Paul commonly referred to as "flesh." We usually use the term *flesh* to refer to the skin that covers our bones. The Bible often uses it this way too. But in Paul's epistles the term *flesh* takes on an additional meaning—our fallen human nature. This is why, as noted in the previous chapter, the New International Version often translates the Greek term for flesh *(sarx)* as "sinful nature" (Romans 7:5, 18, 25; 8:3, 4, 5, 12, 13, etc.), and the New American Standard Bible uses the literal "flesh."

Paul's use of the term *sarx* may have been influenced to some degree by its association with Greek philosophy. Philosophers like Plato viewed the flesh as the lowest part of man and as being subject to lusts that defiled the human soul, which was the higher part of human nature. It is more likely, however, that Paul's view of the flesh was rooted in the Old Testament's theology of sin.

According to the Creation account, the human body was formed from the "dust of the ground" (Genesis 2:7). Dust was a symbol of degradation. According to Genesis 3:14, one aspect of the curse pronounced upon the Serpent after the Fall was that it would "eat dust all the days of [its] life." Dust was also a symbol of that which was common. Abraham and Jacob were promised that their descendants would be as numerous as the dust of the earth (Genesis 13:16; 28:14). After Adam's fall into sin, comparing humanity to dust was a way of pointing out its inherent weakness and transitory nature. When Abraham pleaded with God to spare Sodom, he described himself as "dust and ashes" (Genesis 18:27).

This state of human weakness is something that calls forth compassion from the God who created humanity: "As a father has compassion on his children, so the LORD has compassion on those who fear him; for he knows how we are formed, he remembers that we are dust" (Psalm 103:13–14). The dignity of the human body, therefore, was not derived from its own substance but from the fact that God had breathed the breath of life into it. If anything, the fact that the first human was created from the dust of the earth was meant to underscore the difference between Creator and creature.

One of the consequences of Adam's sin was that the human body became subject to decay and would eventually return to dust (Genesis 3:19). As a result, the Old Testament sometimes uses the term "flesh" in a way that is synonymous with "weakness." For example, when the Lord assessed man's sinful behavior in the days of Noah, He summarized the human condition this way: "Then the LORD said, 'My Spirit will not contend with man forever, for he is mortal [literally "flesh"]; his days will be a hundred and twenty years'" (Genesis 6:3). To be "flesh" is to be weak and in a state of decay. This is why Paul wrote that "flesh and blood cannot inherit the kingdom of God" (1 Corinthians 15:50). The body is perishable by nature and must be made imperishable before it can enjoy the benefits of the kingdom.

A Body Inclined to Disobey God

For Paul, however, the problem of flesh was more than a matter of mere physical weakness and decay. Ultimately, it was a matter of rebellion. Adam's single act of disobedience made a permanent imprint on all of his subsequent descendants. This stamp of sin skewed their thoughts and actions in the direction of disobedience. Paul described his own personal struggle with this sin nature in Romans 7 and characterized it as an internal "law" inclined to do the opposite of whatever God's Law commanded. Good intentions, determination, or sheer human willpower are not enough to overcome the flesh. Only Christ's death and resurrection are strong enough to counter sin's effect upon human nature.

It is the presence of the flesh, the internal sin principle present in every descendant of Adam, that has perverted what was meant to be a holy vessel into a "body of death."

THE CHURCH'S VIEW OF THE BODY

The Gnostics:
Rejecting the Body and the Incarnation

The early church's view of the body was influenced by its struggle with the heresy known as Gnosticism. Gnostic philosophy regarded matter as evil. Marcion, a leading Christian Gnostic of the second century, taught that the material world was the creation of an inferior god. This god placed all of humanity under the bondage of flesh and the burden of law and judgment. Marcion believed that the New Testament revealed a second God who created Jesus Christ. The God of the New Testament was a God of mercy and salvation. The purpose of Christ's work was to free the soul from imprisonment in the body.

Obviously, since Christian Gnostics believed that the body was an inferior mode of existence and evil in nature, they also rejected the doctrine of the Incarnation. Various theories were proposed to explain the apparent humanity of Jesus. Some suggested that Christ merely inhabited the man Jesus, descending upon Him like a dove when He was baptized by John and then abandoning Him once He had completed His mission. Others taught that Christ only appeared to have a human body but that this was not a real body.

Although these views were eventually condemned by the early church, Gnosticism's discomfort with the human body was harder to reject. The body came to be viewed as a potential obstacle to the spiritual life, if not an outright enemy of it. Many early monastics, for example, believed that neglecting the body was a way of strengthening the spirit. Anthony, regarded by many as the father of Christian monasticism, chose to live as a hermit. He often went without sleep, eating just once a day and sometimes only once every other day. He would not eat meat or drink wine and refused to anoint his body with oil. He is said to have declared that the fiber of the soul is healthiest when the pleasures of the body are diminished.

This discomfort with the human body carried over into the Middle Ages. The German mystic Thomas à Kempis (A.D. 1380–1471) wrote a manual of devotion to Christ that is still widely read today. Entitled *The Imitation of Christ,* it said that the physical necessities of the body are a continual source of misery to the devout person. Some even practiced self-inflicted beatings as a way of showing repentance and growing closer to God.

The Reformers:
Restoring Respect for the Body

With the coming of the Renaissance, attitudes toward the human body began to change. Renaissance humanists questioned the spiritual value of asceticism and bodily abuse. Artists began to emphasize the humanity of Christ by portraying His naked body in paintings of the crucifixion.[4] These views affected the Protestant Reformers. In his *Little Catechism,* for example, Martin Luther celebrated God's creation of the human body, as well as His provision for all its material needs.[5]

John Calvin noted the distinction between the body and the soul but emphasized that human nature consisted of both. "The glory of God ought, in some measure, to shine in the several parts of our bodies."[6] In his explanation of the fourth petition of the Lord's Prayer, Calvin rejected the medieval view that believers needed to abuse their bodies in order to become closer to God. When believers ask for their daily bread, they are asking God for everything that their bodies need. Calvin noted that this is not limited only to food and clothing, but includes everything that God perceives to be beneficial to us.

God does not view the human body with contempt. Far from it. "For our most gracious Father does not disdain to take even our bodies under his safekeeping and guardianship in order to exercise our faith in these small matters, while we expect everything from him, even to a crumb of bread and a drop of water," Calvin declared in his *Institutes of the Christian Religion.*[7]

In Modern Times

In the modern era, theologian Karl Barth has described human nature as "bodily soul" and "besouled" body. Although body and soul are not the same, there is a unity between them. In its relation to the body, however, the soul has precedence.[8] Although it is clear from Scripture that the soul affects the body and the body affects the soul, Louis Berkhof has observed, "The exact relation of body and soul to each other has been represented in various ways, but remains to a great extent a mystery."[9]

JESUS AND THE BODY

A Real Body in Birth and Life

The greatest evidence for both the dignity and the spiritual significance of the physical body is found in the Incarnation. At the Incarnation, Jesus Christ, who already existed as God, took to Himself a human nature. One aspect of that nature was a physical body. Colossians 1:22 indicates Christ's "physical" body was the means of the believer's reconciliation to God. Jesus' body was a real human body and not a phantasm. It had all the natural attributes common to us, apart from sin.

For example, although He was miraculously conceived in Mary's womb, the baby Jesus was delivered after the normal period of fetal development (Luke 2:6–7). Jesus' body grew in size and increased in ability. He "grew in wisdom and stature, and in favor with God and men" (Luke 2:52). The fact that Jesus grew in wisdom as well as in stature implies that His growth in knowledge and understanding correlated with His physical development. Like other human infants, Jesus had to learn to walk and talk. His human thought processes developed from simple to more complex.

To borrow Paul's language from a different context, when Jesus was a child He talked like a child, thought like a child, and reasoned like a child. It is true that when Jesus engaged in dialogue with the teachers in the temple, "everyone who heard him was amazed at his understanding and his answers" (Luke 2:47). He was not like any other child they had encountered. He possessed wisdom from God. Yet despite this surprising degree of knowledge, He "grew" in wisdom. The Greek term that is translated "grew" in Luke 2:52 means to "progress" or "advance." Jesus may have been precocious in His knowledge, but He also appears to have been subject to the learning process.

Jesus' body was also subject to ordinary human weaknesses. When it was deprived of food, He became hungry (Matthew 4:2). When it was subjected to physical exertion, He grew weary (John 4:6). Like the rest of us, Jesus slept when He was tired and drank when He was thirsty (Luke 8:23; John 4:6; cf. 19:28). It was a body that could be seen and touched and could only be in one place at a time (John 11:6, 15, 21; 1 John 1:1). According to Matthew 4:5–6, Satan "took" Jesus and "had him stand" on the highest point of the temple in Jerusalem. Then he challenged Jesus to throw Himself down, citing the promise of Psalm 91:11–12 that the angels would lift Him up in their hands to keep Him from being dashed on the stones.

All of this implies that Jesus' body was subject to the normal laws of physics like the law of gravity. Yet because He was God as well as man, Jesus could also choose to act in accordance with His divine nature. Consequently, He was able to walk on water and know what was in the hearts of people without being told (John 6:19; Matthew 9:4).

A Real Body in Resurrection

Jesus continues His bodily existence even though He has been glorified. A bodily form is entirely compatible with His glorified state. When He appeared to His disciples after the Resurrection, He challenged them, saying, "Look at my hands and my feet. It is I myself! Touch me and see; a ghost does not have flesh and bones, as you see I have" (Luke 24:39). Admittedly, there are significant differences in

Christ's postresurrection state. Physical barriers like walls do not seem to be an obstacle for Him. Yet He still possesses a real, physical body.

His body can be touched, and it still bears the marks of His suffering. During one of His postresurrection appearances, Jesus showed Thomas His hands and told him to thrust his finger into His wounds and put his hand into His side (John 20:27).

Eating is another part of the resurrected Christ's bodily experience. One of the ways He proved the reality of His resurrection to the disciples was to eat a piece of fish in front of them (Luke 24:42–43). He also promised His disciples that He would drink of the fruit of the vine with them in the kingdom (Matthew 26:29).

What should we conclude from this? If nothing else, the reality of Christ's physical body shows us that the body does not have to be an enemy of the spiritual life. In fact, for the Christian, spiritual life is an embodied life. Christian spirituality was meant to be expressed in the physical life of the body.

THE SOUL AND THE BODY

A Valued Container

Several years ago someone gave one of my sons a fifty-dollar savings bond for Christmas. The person had placed the bond in an envelope, and my son—who had never received anything like this before—was so eager to open the gift that he tore the envelope in half along with the bond inside. The envelope was only a container for the bond; and between the two, the bond had a much higher value. If only my son had recognized the relationship between the two, he probably would have treated the "container" differently.

The same could be said of the relationship between the body and the soul. There is a sense in which we might view the body as a container for the soul. Between these two, the soul is the more valuable part. Jesus affirmed this in Matthew 10:28 when He warned His disciples: "Do not be afraid of those who kill the body but cannot kill the soul. Rather, be afraid of the One who can destroy both soul and body in hell." The context of this statement had to do with the disciples' proclaiming Christ's teaching and facing possible persecution as a result.

There is a clear order of importance implied in Jesus' words. They suggest that we should be more concerned about the soul than the body. Yet they do not reflect an absolute dichotomy. In this passage, Jesus also linked the fate of the body with that of the soul when He said that God can "destroy both soul and body in hell." He also affirmed the Father's concern for the body when He then added, "Are not two sparrows sold for a penny? Yet not one of them will fall to the ground apart from the will of your Father. And even the very hairs of your head are all numbered. So don't be afraid; you are worth more than many sparrows" (Matthew 10:29–31). It is God's concern (and ultimate control) over my body that serves as the motivation for not giving in to my fear of those who can only destroy the flesh.

A Vital Connection

Yet if the body is a "container" for the soul, it is more than a mere shell. There is a vital connection between the two. The most obvious connection is that the soul animates the body. The origin of the human soul is described in Genesis 2:7. When God breathed the breath of life into Adam's nostrils, "man became a living being." The Hebrew term translated "being" in this verse is *nephesh,* a word that is sometimes translated "soul." When the soul departs, death comes to the body (Genesis 35:18). The term *nephesh* is often used in a way that is synonymous with the Hebrew word *ruach* or "spirit." For example, the psalmist warns against putting trust in princes rather than in God because princes are mere mortals who cannot save. "When their spirit departs," the psalmist explains, "they return to the ground; on that very day their plans come to nothing" (Psalm 146:4). Likewise, the author of the book of Ecclesiastes alludes to man's creation from the dust of the earth when he says that "the dust returns to the ground it came from, and the spirit returns to God who gave it" (Ecclesiastes 12:7).

The New Testament uses similar language. In the New Testament the Greek term *pneuma* is used to refer to the spirit. In Luke's account of the raising of the daughter of Jairus, the text says that when Jesus restored her to life, "her spirit returned, and at once she stood up" (Luke 8:55). Just prior to His death, Jesus prayed these words: "Father, into your hands I commit my spirit" (Luke 23:46). When He died, He "bowed his head and gave up his spirit" (John 19:30). This language is not exclusive to Jesus. As Stephen was being stoned to death, he prayed, "Lord Jesus, receive my spirit" (Acts 7:59). According to James 2:26, "The body without the spirit is dead."

The fact that at death the soul or spirit returns to God while the body returns to the dust indicates that the soul can exist apart from the body. Although the body may cease to function, the soul does not. Ultimately it is the presence of the soul that makes you a living being and not the state of your body. Consequently, you are more than a body. This is certainly an important reminder for a culture as obsessed with body image as ours. Our sense of self-worth and the value we place on others are often directly related to physical appearance.

The Soul's Proper Priority

Yet the priority of the soul and its eternal nature should force us to look beyond the state of the physical body when determining human value or defining what constitutes a "living being." Biblically speaking, life is more than either consciousness or functionality. One can be unconscious and yet still be alive. Someone in a deep coma, although unconscious, is still a person. One whose body has been so damaged that it can no longer function normally—a quadriplegic or even someone in a vegetative state, for example—is no less a person than an Olympic athlete. It is the presence of the soul that makes us living beings.

But what happens to the status of the body once the soul is absent? In his book *On Being Human,* Ray S. Anderson observed, "The soul is not an abstract concept which is located in a concrete place—the body. Rather, the soul is the life of that particular body, which is the person. If it were not the body of the soul, it would not be a body, but merely a material or even organic thing—a corpse."[10] If the body is only material, it need not be afforded the dignity of a person. It can be treated like matter.

This is of particular importance when we consider more complex issues like the rights of the unborn, the question of euthanasia, and even the practice of transplanting organs from one person to another. As long as the soul is present, the body must be treated with the respect that is due a person. The difficulty, of course, would seem to be in knowing at what point the presence of the soul begins or ends. There is no known instrument capable of measuring the soul's presence.

Yet the question may be easier to answer than we think. The Bible is clear on one point, at least. The body is dead without the soul. As long as there is physical life, regardless of the "quality" of that life, the soul is present. Although we may never be able to identify the exact moment that the soul leaves, we can be certain that when life is no longer sustained, the soul has departed from the body.

HOW THE BODY AFFECTS THE SOUL

It is equally important to note that while the presence of the soul gives life to the body, the behavior of the body affects the soul. The Scriptures seem to indicate that the body becomes uninhabitable by the soul when its physical state declines to the point of death. To use the language of the King James Version, at that point the body "yields the ghost" (that is, the soul or spirit; cf. Matthew 27:50). Mistreatment of the body, whether it is my mistreatment of my own body or my mistreatment of someone else's body, as well as simple physical decline, has the potential to "dispossess" the soul.

The Body: An Instrument for Good or Evil

However, the connection between body and soul is not just a matter of dwelling space—or perhaps more accurately "dwelling place," as the soul's relationship to the body is not spatial. There is a qualitative connection between the two. The actions of the body have spiritual and moral implications for the life of the soul. It is possible to use the body in a way that defiles the soul. Jesus used extraordinarily strong language in the Sermon on the Mount to warn about the spiritual implications of the body when He said, "If your right eye causes you to sin, gouge it out and throw it away. It is better for you to lose one part of your body than for your whole body to be thrown into hell. And if your right hand causes you to sin, cut it off and throw it away. It is better for you to lose one part of your body than for your whole body to go into hell" (Matthew 5:29–30).

Obviously, Jesus did not expect His disciples to take this counsel literally. His use of hyperbolic language was meant to underscore the importance of making every effort to deal with sin. Yet by warning that the "whole body" may be thrown into hell as a result of the action of one of its members, Jesus acknowledged that the way one uses the body affects the moral state of the whole person. Later in this Sermon on the Mount, Jesus even ascribed moral characteristics to the body itself, not just to its actions. According to Matthew 6:22–23, one's eye can either be "good" or "evil." Like the previous passage, this was a figure of speech meant to drive home the danger of sin. In this case the eye reflects the moral character of the inner person. In 2 Corinthians 7:1 the apostle Paul spoke of our need to "purify ourselves from everything that contaminates body and spirit."

These statements underscore the solidarity that exists between body and soul. The body does not act independently. Its behavior is a reflection of the soul. The current of moral behavior primarily moves from the inside out—from soul to body—and only secondarily in the other direction. If there are times when the functions of the body seem to have a life of their own, such as those occasions when we are troubled by sinful inclinations that go against our internal desire to act in a godly way, it is only because the body is responding to the impulses of the sinful nature. Paul describes these impulses as a "law of sin" at work within the members of one's body that makes the individual its prisoner (Romans 7:23).

The hope of the believer is that the redemptive work of Christ has introduced a new law within that is capable of counteracting this internal law (Romans 8:2–4). Consequently, Paul describes the Christian life as one of "perfecting holiness out of reverence for God" (2 Corinthians 7:1). This perfecting process begins with the recognition that God has a claim upon my body. Yes, I exercise a degree of freedom in my use of it, but it does not really belong to me. The freedom I exercise over my body is the freedom of stewardship.

The Body: The Machinery of Holiness

So where does the body figure in the life of discipleship? It serves as the machinery of holiness. Our bodies are the instruments we employ to worship and serve God. My body was purchased by Christ's death, and its purpose is to glorify God. "Do you not know that your body is a temple of the Holy Spirit, who is in you, whom you have received from God? You are not your own; you were bought at a price. Therefore honor God with your body" (1 Corinthians 6:19–20).

Every human body is sacred because it is the dwelling place of the soul. But the Christian's body is doubly sacred because it is both the dwelling place of the human soul and the temple of the Holy Spirit.

Paul describes the believer's use of the body with two primary metaphors—sacrifice and slavery. The Christian's obligation is to "offer" the body as a living sacrifice (Romans 12:1). The alternative is to "offer" the members of our body "in slavery to impurity and to ever-increasing wickedness" (Romans 6:19). The dominant idea in both cases is that of "offering" or "presenting." The same term *(paristemi)* is used in both Romans 12:1 and Romans 6:19 and points simultaneously to the voluntary and submissive nature of the action it describes. For Christians, the choice either to use the body to serve God or to serve sin is a voluntary one. That is because the work of Christ has given us a freedom that we did not previously possess. We who are in Christ "have been set free from sin" (Romans 6:22). We now have the liberty to place our bodies at God's disposal. It is the freedom to acknowledge that we are Christ's servants.

Despite this freedom, we may still choose to serve sin. We are no longer its slaves but may choose to live in voluntary servitude to it. This is the case every time we make the choice to sin: "Don't you know that when you offer yourselves to someone to obey him as slaves, you are slaves to the one whom you obey—whether you are slaves to sin, which leads to death, or to obedience, which leads to righteousness?" (Romans 6:16). Prior to Christ we were slaves to sin. This meant that we were "free from the control of righteousness" (Romans 6:20). When we offer our bodies to God we offer them "in slavery to righteousness leading to holiness" (Romans 6:19).

GOD'S PURPOSE FOR THE BODY

The Eyes Have It

Several of the body's members are the focus of statements in Scripture. As has already been noted, Jesus spoke of the possibility of the eye causing one to sin (Matthew 5:29), of acting, as it were, like "an evil eye." Jesus also warned that anyone who looks at another person with lust has already committed adultery of the heart (Matthew 5:28). More often, however, the Bible warns of what the eye implies about the inner person.

This is especially true of the book of Proverbs. A scoundrel is someone who "winks with his eye" (Proverbs 6:13; cf. 16:30). "Haughty" eyes are one of the things that God finds detestable (Proverbs 6:16–17). Along with a proud heart, haughty eyes are called "the lamp of the wicked" (Proverbs 21:4). The adulteress captivates her unsuspecting victims with her eyes (Proverbs 6:25). A fool's eyes "wander to the ends of the earth" but the wise person "keeps wisdom in view" (Proverbs 17:24).

However, not everything the Bible says about the eyes is evil. They can be used for good as well. When the king sits on his throne to judge, "he winnows out all evil with his eyes" (Proverbs 20:8).

What the Ears Hear

The ear is also important. Wisdom is gained by turning one's ear to it (Proverbs 2:2). The wicked shut their ears to the cry of the poor, but the wise will apply their "heart to instruction and [their] ears to

words of knowledge" (Proverbs 21:13; 23:12). A "listening ear" is one
that is quick to pay attention to the lesson of a wise man's rebuke and
is compared to an earring of gold (Proverbs 25:12). The prophet
Isaiah acknowledges that God "morning by morning, wakens my ear
to listen like one being taught. The Sovereign LORD has opened my
ears, and I have not been rebellious; I have not drawn back" (50:4–5).
However, someone who turns a "deaf ear" to God's Law will find that
his prayers are "detestable" (Proverbs 28:9).

The prophet Jeremiah characterized the house of Jacob as a "foolish and senseless people, who have eyes but do not see, who have ears
but do not hear" (Jeremiah 5:21). This biblical emphasis on being wise
listeners was echoed in the ministry of Christ Himself. Repeatedly
Jesus urged: "He who has an ear, let him hear" (Matthew 11:15; 13:9,
43; Mark 4:9, 23; Luke 8:8; 14:35; cf. Revelation 2:7, 3:6, 13, 22;
13:9). Stephen accused his contemporaries of having "uncircumcised
hearts and ears" and of resisting the Holy Spirit (Acts 7:51).

Tongues That Bless or Curse

The tongue can be either an instrument of blessing or of cursing.
The prophet Isaiah said that God had given him both a listening ear
and an instructed tongue: "The Sovereign LORD has given me an instructed tongue, to know the word that sustains the weary. . . . wakens
my ear to listen like one being taught" (Isaiah 50:4). The tongue, however, can be used for evil or good. It has as much power to destroy as
it does to heal. (See, for example, Proverbs 10:20–21; 12:18; 18:21.)

Yet knowing when not to use the tongue can be as important as
speaking wisely (Proverbs 11:12). In the New Testament, James identifies the ability to control the tongue as one of the benchmarks of
spiritual maturity. "If anyone considers himself religious and yet does
not keep a tight rein on his tongue," he warns, "he deceives himself and
his religion is worthless" (James 1:26). Despite its small size, the
tongue has almost unlimited potential for damage. It is described as
"a fire," "a world of evil among the parts of the body," and has the potential to "corrupt the whole person" (James 3:6).

Keeping Our Hands Clean,
Our Feet Moving Forward

King David declared that only those who have "clean" hands may come into God's presence (Psalm 24:4). Bloodthirsty men, however, are those "in whose hands are wicked schemes, whose right hands are full of bribes" (Psalm 26:10). Hands can be lifted up in prayer or in anger (1 Timothy 2:8). Christians are encouraged to make their ambition to lead a quiet life and to work with their hands (1 Thessalonians 4:11).

Feet, like one's hands and tongue, can be used as much for evil purposes as for good. The wicked use their feet to "rush into sin" (Proverbs 1:16; 6:18). Yet they can also be used to bring the message of the gospel to others (Romans 10:15).

THE BODY IS FOR THE LORD

How important is the body? It is important enough to comprise the capstone of the believer's redemptive experience. The Scriptures teach that bodily resurrection is the inevitable result of being united with Christ (Romans 6:5). The corruptible bodies we now inhabit are destined to be transformed. "Now we know that if the earthly tent we live in is destroyed, we have a building from God, an eternal house in heaven, not built by human hands" (2 Corinthians 5:1). Consequently, our present state is one of longing for the resurrection body. The soul's ultimate desire is not to be a disembodied spirit, but to be "clothed" with an imperishable body. This was the purpose for which we were made (2 Corinthians 5:4–5).

Such hope provides the proper theological perspective with regard to our earthly bodies. God's purpose for our earthly body is the same as His purpose for our "heavenly" body: Both are created for His glory. To use Paul's language, "The body is . . . for the Lord, and the Lord for the body" (1 Corinthians 6:13).

This was an issue in the church of Corinth because some had concluded that it did not matter how one treated the physical body since it was merely physical and would one day be destroyed. They believed that God was indifferent to the believer's use of the body. Their own behavior was guided by such slogans as "Everything is permissible for me" and "Food for the stomach and the stomach for food." Paul affirmed the reality of the believer's liberty in Christ but noted that it is a liberty that is limited by two important boundaries. The first boundary is set by the potential effect of a behavior. What is legally permissible (i.e., not explicitly forbidden in Scripture) may not be beneficial. If so, it is to be avoided. The second boundary is the limit set by the potential for "mastery." "Everything is permissible for me," Paul acknowledged, "but I will not be mastered by anything" (1 Corinthians 6:12).

Although eating and drinking will still have a place in our eternal experience, their function will be changed (Matthew 26:29; Revelation 19:9). Food and drink will no longer be the primary means of sustaining the body. The stomach is only temporary, but this is not true of the body.

When I was a student in seminary, a chapel speaker preached a message with Romans 12:1 as the text but spent most of the hour criticizing Christians who were overweight. "How can you tell the unsaved that Jesus will help them overcome their sin," he thundered, "when you can't even control what you put in your mouth!" A thin man himself, he looked as if he had never had to worry about being overweight.

In the class that followed, we asked our professor, whose body type did not reflect the "slim, firm, and disciplined" ideal that the speaker had been advocating with such vehemence, his opinion of the sermon. He looked down at the floor with a mischievous smile and folded his hands over his own considerable girth. "Well," he rumbled, "all I know is that the Bible says that the 'liberal soul shall be made fat!'" (See Proverbs 11:25 KJV.)

What kind of body does God prefer? Ultimately it is not a question of size or shape but of consecration. The primary function of the body is not to be put on display but to be offered to God as a living sacrifice. We were created to worship and serve God with our bodies. Both now and in eternity, the body is for the Lord.

GOD'S
GYM

TRAINING
FOR GODLINESS

In my senior year of high school I joined the track team. But I never placed first . . . or second . . . or third, for that matter. In fact, I spent most track meets standing on the sidelines watching others run. This was not by my own choice. The coaches did not ask me to race very often because I wasn't likely to win.

They did try to help me, though. During practice they had me experiment with a variety of events, each with the same lackluster result. Finally, one of them suggested that I try throwing the shot put. It seemed to me to be an ideal choice. It didn't involve any running. Instead, all I had to do was spin around in a circle and heave something that looked like a small cannonball as far as I could. How difficult could it be? Much harder than I thought, it turned out. Because no matter how much effort I put into it or how far I tried to hurl it, the shot put always seemed to fall with a dull thud a few inches from where I stood.

After I had made a few attempts, the coach tried to encourage me. "It's a shame you didn't come out for the team a few years ago. I think you could have been pretty good at this." At first I was puzzled by his comment. *If I'm this bad now,* I reasoned, *I would have been just as bad then. What difference would a year or two make?* The answer, I now realize, was in the training. For most of that season I thought that my problem was that I wasn't a natural athlete. The real reason was that I hadn't had much training and that when I had trained I hadn't tried very hard. It was training that made the others more successful.

Could the same be true of the spiritual life as well? Do we believe that spiritual maturity is something that some people just "have" and others don't? Or do training and sustained efforts also contribute to our spiritual development? We know that God is the ultimate source of spiritual life and that His Spirit produces the fruit that is the measure of spiritual maturity (Galatians 5:22). Yet the Bible also compares the disciple of Christ to an athlete in training.

"Have nothing to do with godless myths and old wives' tales; rather, train yourself to be godly. For physical training is of some value, but godliness has value for all things, holding promise for both the present life and the life to come" (1 Timothy 4:7–8). The Greek term that is translated "train" in this verse is also the term from which we get the word *gymnasium.* It literally meant "to exercise." But Paul was not referring to physical exercise, which has value only in the present, but to spiritual exercise. Its goal is to produce a certain kind of behavior that produces benefits both in the present and in eternity. The value of spiritual exercise is that it has the potential to produce godliness.

THE GOAL OF SPIRITUAL TRAINING: GODLY BEHAVIOR

Godly Versus Ungodly Behavior

Several New Testament epistles address godliness as a characteristic of the believer, particularly Paul's two letters to Timothy, his letter to Titus, and Peter's second letter. Yet they often do not give a detailed definition of what is meant by the term. What does a "godly" person look like?

One way to answer this question is by comparing godliness to its opposite. For example, Paul notes that one of the primary marks of godlessness is to "suppress the truth" by unrighteous behavior ("wickedness," Romans 1:18). Godliness, then, must have the opposite effect. Godly behavior brings the truth to light. Godliness has its origin in God's truth. Those who occupy themselves with what Paul describes as "godless chatter" will "become more and more ungodly." They will deviate from the fundamental principles of the faith (2 Timothy 2:16–18; cf. 1 Timothy 6:20). Godliness, on the other hand, is built upon the foundation of the word of truth (2 Timothy 2:15).

Knowledge of the truth leads to godliness (Titus 1:1). That is why the command to train for godliness in 1 Timothy 4:7 is immediately preceded by a warning to avoid "godless myths and old wives' tales." In Paul's day, these myths were the products of false teachers who promoted a spirituality of asceticism. They forbade marriage and ordered people to abstain from certain foods (1 Timothy 4:3). If true godliness is the opposite of this, it must be a kind of holiness that can be reflected in the ordinary pursuits of life. It is as much at home in the family and at the dinner table as it is in the sanctuary.

Ungodly behavior is also profane. It has no regard for the sacred. It is the attitude of Esau, "who for a single meal sold his inheritance rights as the oldest son" (Hebrews 12:16). Esau was a sensualist at heart, driven by his appetite to such a degree that he was willing to sell his inheritance for a single meal. "His foolishness in exchanging his privilege as the eldest son for a single meal is so glaring," commentator Donald Guthrie observed, "that he has become the type of all who put material or sensual advantages before their spiritual heritage."[1]

The godly person knows the value of God's promises and will not barter them for profit or pleasure, no matter how immediate either may be. In this same verse in Hebrews, the writer warns his readers to look carefully to make sure that no one in their midst shares Esau's godless values. This is a responsibility shared by the entire congregation. Godliness flourishes best in an environment of loving accountability.

Saying Yes to God

One of the most important characteristics of the godly person is the ability to say no to the flesh and yes to God. Titus 2:11–14 says that the grace of God "teaches us to say 'No' to ungodliness and worldly passions, and to live self-controlled, upright and godly lives in this present age, while we wait for the blessed hope—the glorious appearing of our great God and Savior, Jesus Christ, who gave himself for us to redeem us from all wickedness and to purify for himself a people that are his very own, eager to do what is good." Although the godly person is not immune to the tug of sin, he or she has learned to renounce it. This is both the result of a definitive commitment made in the past and a growing understanding gained from the lessons that are being learned as the person lives the Christian life in the present.

Those who know Christ as Savior have entered God's training program and are currently under the instructional care of the grace of God. They are teachable and willing to redirect their thinking and actions when corrected by the truth of Scripture or the conviction of the Holy Spirit. Learning the lessons of grace and saying no to the flesh both require a certain type of thinking. It is the kind of thinking that the Bible often characterizes as "temperate," "self-controlled," or "clear minded" thinking (1 Timothy 3:2; Titus 2:2; 1 Peter 4:7). Such thinking makes one aware of his own strengths and weaknesses. It is firmly rooted in God's promise of grace that will overcome the pull of the flesh.

Eyeing the Future

The godly person has an eye on the future. The disciple's hope is fixed on "the glorious appearing of our great God and Savior, Jesus Christ." It might be expected that this focus would lead to an unhealthy "otherworldliness," the kind of attitude that leaves Christians so heavenly minded that they are no earthly good. Yet Titus 2:14 indicates that it has the opposite effect. It makes the believer "eager to do what is good." Someone who is godly is able to live in two worlds simultaneously. He or she is a citizen of heaven who is in pilgrimage on the earth. Disciples who have set their hope on Christ's coming are eager for Christ's return, willing to abstain from sinful desires, and careful in the way that they live before those who do not believe (Philippians 3:20; 1 Peter 2:11–12).

Disciples of Jesus know that God is watching and that when Christ returns to judge the earth, "everything in it will be laid bare" (2 Peter 3:10). This sense of impending judgment is a strong motivation for godly living in the present. "Since everything will be destroyed in this way, what kind of people ought you to be? You ought to live holy and godly lives as you look forward to the day of God and speed its coming. That day will bring about the destruction of the heavens by fire, and the elements will melt in the heat" (2 Peter 3:11–12).

THE MEANS OF SPIRITUAL TRAINING: GRACE, TRUTH, AND EFFORT

Godliness is the goal of spiritual training, but what are the tools God uses to produce it in the believer? The three primary instruments of training are grace, truth, and divinely empowered effort. Most important of these is the grace of God.

God's Grace to Us

Grace is the ground for all godliness. There is no godliness without grace. In fact, if the foundation of God's grace is removed, the same actions that are a reflection of godliness in the believer become a form of ungodliness. Our own self-righteousness distorts them. God has saved us and called us to live a holy life, "not because of anything we have done but because of his own purpose and grace" (2 Timothy 1:9). Once we have trusted in Christ, it is the grace of God that "teaches us to say 'No' to ungodliness and worldly passions" (Titus 2:12). The grace of God gives us the confidence to resist the flesh and the devil because it assures us that when we draw near to God in repentance, He will draw near to us (James 4:6–8).

Grace is also at the root of our eagerness to see Jesus Christ return because we expect to receive even more grace when we see Him. According to the apostle Peter, this expectation of future grace is what motivates us to lead a holy life. "Therefore, prepare your minds for action; be self-controlled; set your hope fully on the grace to be given you when Jesus Christ is revealed. As obedient children, do not conform to the evil desires you had when you lived in ignorance. But just as he who called you is holy, so be holy in all you do; for it is written: 'Be holy, because I am holy'" (1 Peter 1:13–16).

The Christian life begins in grace, it will be completed in grace, but it is also lived out in grace. Grace is a dynamic that works in our lives even now. One theologian has defined grace as "the redeeming activity of God."[2] As such, it is not limited to the point of salvation alone. It is a part of every aspect of the redemptive experience. That means that after we have been saved by grace, we must also serve by grace. It is God's grace that empowers us to obey. It equips us for service (1 Corinthians 15:10). Whenever we exercise spiritual gifts, we function as stewards of God's grace because it is God working through us. "Each one should use whatever gift he has received to serve others, faithfully administering God's grace in its various forms" (1 Peter 4:10). Grace even supplies us with the means and the desire to give generously (2 Corinthians 9:7–8).

Truth and Grace

As important as grace is, however, it does not operate alone. The handmaid of grace is truth. If there is no godliness without grace, it must also be said that there is no grace without truth. In the Christian life neither functions without the other. Jesus Himself epitomized this reality. He was "full of grace and truth" (John 1:14). The apostle John summarized Jesus' ministry by saying that the Law came through Moses, but "grace and truth came through Jesus Christ" (John 1:17).

Jesus said that He was "the way and the truth and the life" (John 14:6). We often use this verse to prove that the gospel is objectively and absolutely true. But William Willimon, dean of the chapel at Duke

University, has warned that using such terminology may also inadvertently minimize the role of grace in the Christian experience. "Arguing that Christ and his way are 'objectively true,' we run the risk of deceiving people into thinking that they are capable, just as they are, of thinking about these matters without first knowing Jesus, without conversion."[3] Since the fall of Adam, our natural inclination is to "exchange the truth for a lie" (Romans 1:25). "There is a sense," Willimon explained, "in which we cannot know the truth without first being made truthful."[4]

If this is so, truth alone will not help us. We need both grace and truth. An unbeliever cannot come to faith in Christ by reason alone. The mind is "unspiritual" apart from the intervention of God's grace (Colossians 2:18). It has been blinded by Satan (2 Corinthians 4:4). The unregenerate mind can think about God, study the Scriptures, and even engage in religious activity. Yet its thinking is "futile" because it is given to empty speculation about God (Ephesians 4:17). Those who have not experienced the grace of God are "darkened in their understanding and separated from the life of God because of the ignorance that is in them due to the hardening of their hearts" (Ephesians 4:18). Notice that the root of their ignorance is not so much intellectual as it is volitional. There is more to their ignorance than a lack of information. It is their own hard heartedness that leads to spiritual blindness. Spiritual blindness in turn produces moral impurity (v. 19).

Yet God has chosen to reveal the very grace that the unbeliever needs in propositional form. For us to become truthful, as Willimon argued, grace is conveyed through a message of truth that is couched in human language and addresses both the mind and the heart. Once that message has been received by faith, the transformation of the believer's life comes as a result of "renewing" the mind (Romans 12:2). In both cases, God is working through the Holy Spirit in concert with the truth of Scripture. Consequently, Paul said that the Colossian believers "understood God's grace in all its truth" (Colossians 1:5). Their experience was both rational and spiritual. The proclamation of the truth addressed the mind, while the Holy Spirit filled the Colossians with the knowledge of God's will and with spiritual understanding

(Colossians 1:9). According to New Testament commentator H. C. G. Moule, "The Colossians had not only heard and, in a natural sense, understood the Gospel; they had seen into it with the intuition of grace."[5]

Fundamentally only the transforming power of the grace of God in Christ can explain the difference between the Christian and the unbeliever. But God's grace does not circumvent the learning process. Before we can act upon God's gracious promises, we must first hear the truth about our position in Christ and our new nature. We must be taught to "put off the old self" and "put on the new" (Ephesians 4:21–24). This means that the spiritual life must of necessity also be a life of the mind. The mind plays a critical role in the Christian's spiritual development. J. P. Moreland, professor of philosophy at Biola University, wrote, "The mind is the soul's primary vehicle for making contact with God, and it plays a fundamental role in the process of human maturation and change, including spiritual transformation."[6]

The Role of Effort

Divinely empowered effort is the third factor that contributes to the believer's spiritual development. Human effort is as necessary to spiritual growth as grace and truth. Grace supplies the enabling power and the potential for transformation. Truth provides the direction. But what Christ has made possible must be actualized in human experience by effort. When he was asked if only a few would be saved, Jesus urged His listeners to "make every effort" to enter through the narrow door of salvation (Luke 13:24). The Greek term that appears in this verse was used outside the New Testament in contexts that spoke of doing battle, competing in athletic contests, and of moral striving. Commentator I. Howard Marshall notes that this statement stresses that "moral effort is necessary to enter the kingdom."[7]

At first glance, this might seem to contradict the Bible's teaching elsewhere that grace is the basis of our salvation (Ephesians 2:9–10). Yet Jesus does not say that the way to be saved is to try hard enough to be "good." The "moral effort" mentioned by Jesus is focused on entering by the narrow gate. Ultimately, it is one's choice of Christ that ensures salvation, not whether one has worked hard enough at being a moral person. The experience of God's compassion does not depend upon our effort or even upon our own desire, but upon God's mercy (Romans 9:15–16).

The language of effort is also used in passages that refer to the responsibilities that come as a part of the Christian life. In these passages the grace-driven effort that produces spiritual growth falls into four major categories. *First, there is the effort of resistance.* Because of the presence of the flesh, spiritual growth does not come without a struggle. "Where there is grace," J. C. Ryle warned, "there will be conflict. The believer is a soldier. There is no holiness without warfare. Saved souls will always be found to have fought a fight."[8] The entrance of God's grace actually introduces conflict into the Christian's life because it also introduces the presence of the Holy Spirit. The sinful nature and the Holy Spirit are always in conflict with one another (Galatians 5:17). Sinful desires war against the soul (1 Peter 2:11). The presence of grace does not make obedience to God easy or even natural. Instead, it creates the potential for struggle and eventual victory over the sinful nature.

The second category of grace-driven effort is the positive effort of pursuit. Spiritual growth requires focus. The Scriptures instruct us to "make every effort" and to "pursue" peace, righteousness, godliness, faith, love, endurance, and gentleness (Romans 14:19; 1 Timothy 6:11; 2 Timothy 2:22; Hebrews 12:14; 1 Peter 3:11). The Greek term used in these verses conveys the idea of following or running after something.

The third category of commands emphasizes initiative. Second Peter 1:5–7, for example, contains a list of virtues like goodness, knowledge, self-control, perseverance, godliness, brotherly kindness, and love, along with the command to "make every effort" to add these to our faith. Likewise, Peter writes that we should "make every effort to be found spotless, blameless and at peace with [God]" (2 Peter 3:14). In these verses the Greek term translated "make every effort" is a word that is often used in contexts that speak of zeal or intense activity.

The fourth category of grace-driven effort involves imitating others who serve as spiritual mentors and role models. In 1 Corinthians 4:16 the apostle Paul urged the Corinthians to imitate his example. To help them in this, he sent Timothy, whose example would serve as a reminder of Paul's way of life (1 Corinthians 4:17). Paul repeats this command in 1 Corinthians 11:1: "Follow my example, as I follow the example of Christ." In effect, Paul told the Corinthians to imitate Christ by imitating Timothy who was imitating Paul! The author of the book of Hebrews commanded his readers to imitate those who had first preached the gospel to them (Hebrews 13:7).

THE METHOD OF SPIRITUAL TRAINING:
SPIRITUAL EXERCISES

In all of these passages, the weight of responsibility appears to be placed upon the shoulders of the believer. The Scriptures exhort the disciple to take the initiative and make an effort. If the virtues and actions described in them were automatic, they would be stated as promises rather than commands.

So how should we understand Paul's warning elsewhere that human effort is not the cause of spiritual development? "Are you so foolish?" he asks in Galatians 3:3. "After beginning with the Spirit, are you now trying to attain your goal by human effort?" Is effort incompatible with grace?

Effort is incompatible with grace when that effort is seen as a means of earning God's acceptance. When my efforts become the basis for my confidence with God, rather than the work of Christ, I have crossed over into the realm of legalism. In such a case, however, the problem is not with the effort itself, so much as it is with the notion of earning that accompanies it.

Grace and effort are compatible when grace is itself the basis for effort. That is why Peter's command in 2 Peter 1:5 to "add" virtues like goodness, knowledge, self-control and perseverance to our lives is immediately preceded by the reminder that it is God's own power that has "given us everything we need for life and godliness" (v. 3).

Training and Practice

Grace-driven effort is essential to spiritual development. But what kind of effort is most effective? In his book *The Spirit of the Disciplines,* Dallas Willard suggests that many Christians fail in obedience because they fail to train for obedience. "It is part of the misguided and whimsical condition of humankind," he observes, "that we so devoutly believe in the power of effort-at-the-moment-of-action alone to accomplish what we want and completely ignore the character of change in our lives as a whole."[9] He compares this to an aspiring baseball player who tries to imitate a favorite star, without engaging in the same kind of life preparation and training that enables the professional athlete to perform with seemingly effortless skill during the game. "A baseball player who expects to excel in the game without adequate exercise of his body," Willard warns, "is no more ridiculous than the Christian who hopes to be able to act in the manner of Christ when put to the test without the appropriate exercise in godly living."[10]

The secret, then, is not mere effort; it is effort empowered by the Holy Spirit. But more than that, success in the spiritual life requires prepared effort. Living like Christ does not come automatically once we have placed our faith in the Savior. Spiritual maturity demands training and practice. The way we prepare to live the Christian life is by practicing the spiritual disciplines.

Discipline More than Mere Exercise

If you are like me, however, the thought that spiritual growth demands discipline can be discouraging. A few years ago my wife and I decided that I needed an exercise program, so we purchased a rowing machine. I tried it a few times, but when I was finished my back hurt. I kept telling myself that "someday" I would be disciplined enough to exercise on it regularly, but it remained tucked away in a storage room in my basement gathering dust.

A few years later, I bought a stationary bike. This seemed like a better choice than the rowing machine. At least it wouldn't hurt my back.

I was determined to exercise daily on the bike when I purchased it. But like the rowing machine, it was soon sitting neglected in a basement corner. Well, not exactly neglected—we did hang our laundry on it!

If spiritual growth comes as a result of planned effort, is there any hope for those like you and me? The good news is that our success in practicing the spiritual disciplines does not depend upon our ability to be regular in our regimen of physical exercises.

"A disciplined person is not simply someone who exercises many disciplines," John Ortberg clarifies. "A disciplined person is not a highly systematic, rigidly scheduled, chart-marking, gold-star-loving early riser. The Pharisees were rigid and organized, but they were not disciplined persons in the sense required by true discipleship."[11]

What, then, is the secret to successful spiritual discipline? It is largely a matter of having the right motive and employing the right means.

Having the Right Motive

One of the worst motives for engaging in spiritual training is pride. Jesus condemned many of the religious leaders of His day for practicing spiritual disciplines purely for the sake of being seen by others (Matthew 6:5–7, 17–18). Jesus told His disciples that they were to be different. "Be careful not to do your 'acts of righteousness' before men, to be seen by them," He warned. "If you do, you will have no reward from your Father in heaven" (Matthew 6:1). This is not a criticism of public acts of righteousness. Elsewhere Jesus told the disciples, "Let your light shine before men, that they may see your good deeds and praise your Father in heaven" (Matthew 5:16). It is the purpose rather than the practice that creates the difficulty.

As someone who has trusted in Jesus Christ, I should do acts of righteousness. Others should be able to see that righteousness. But if my motive is to be seen by others, then what may appear to be righteousness isn't righteousness at all. It is hypocrisy because all my outward acts are a sham. They appear to be directed toward God, when in reality I don't care about what God thinks at all.

So why should we train for righteousness? Generally for the same reason we engage in physical discipline—because we benefit from result: "Have nothing to do with godless myths and old wives' tales; rather, train yourself to be godly. For physical training is of some value, but godliness has value for all things, holding promise for both the present life and the life to come" (1 Timothy 4:7–8).

FOUNDATIONAL DISCIPLINES

Once I know that my motives are right, I have another decision to make. Which disciplines should I practice? There are many from which to choose. If we accept John Ortberg's definition that a spiritual discipline is "any activity that can help me to gain power to live life as Jesus taught and modeled it,"[12] then almost any action can serve as a spiritual discipline under the right circumstances. In the practice of the New Testament church, however, four disciplines surface as being foundational to spiritual growth. They are mentioned in Acts 2:42, which says that the early disciples "devoted themselves to the apostles' teaching and to the fellowship, to the breaking of bread and to prayer."

1. Teaching

First on the list is "the apostles' teaching." This is more than simply studying Scripture. It refers to doctrinal instruction. The study of doctrine has fallen out of favor among some Christians today because it is seen as potentially divisive. They believe that it is an obstacle to vibrant Christian practice. Their attitude is like that of the Sunday school teacher who warned me not to go to seminary. He called it "cemetery" and warned that it would quench my zeal for Christ. Others go to the opposite extreme. They are very interested in doctrine but not as concerned about practice. For them, Christianity is mostly a matter of believing the right doctrine.

The Bible's approach to doctrine is more balanced. It emphasizes both doctrine and practice. Christian doctrine is the truth that guides the disciple's practice, and Christian practice is really applied doctrine: "All Scripture is God-breathed and is useful for teaching, rebuking, correcting and training in righteousness, so that the man of God may be thoroughly equipped for every good work" (2 Timothy 3:16–17).

2. Fellowship

The New Testament church also engaged in "fellowship." This Greek term literally meant "sharing." New Testament believers experienced this sharing in many different ways. They shared a common faith in Christ and had all experienced the baptism of the Holy Spirit (Philippians 2:1). In practical terms this "fellowship" was expressed by sharing their material goods with other poor believers (Acts 2:44–45; Romans 15:26; 2 Corinthians 8:4).

Fellowship is the experience of union that believers enjoy because of common ground they experience in Christ. It is the sense of togetherness that makes the church we attend "our" church and reminds us that those we worship with are brothers and sisters in Christ.

The experience of Christian fellowship, however, is not limited to our own church or circle of friends. It is something that we have in common with all believers. The apostle Paul saw this demonstrated in a vivid and practical way when the Macedonian churches chose, despite their own poverty, to send a generous offering to the suffering church in Jerusalem. They gave out of "the most severe trial" and "extreme poverty" because they were motivated by "overflowing joy" (2 Corinthians 8:2). Aware of their poverty, Paul had tried to talk them out of giving but they had pleaded with him "for the privilege of sharing in this service to the saints" (v. 4).

3. Breaking of Bread

Christian fellowship was symbolized in the "breaking of bread." The only other place where this phrase appears in the New Testament is in Luke 24:35, where it refers to Jesus breaking the bread at a meal with the two disciples who met Him on the road to Emmaus. In Acts

2:42 it may mean only that the disciples ate their meals together. It is more likely, however, that it refers to the ordinance of the Lord's Supper. During the first century the church often observed the Lord's Supper in connection with a congregational meal or "Love Feast"(cf. 1 Corinthians 11:20–21).

When we celebrate the Lord's Supper together, we remember the price that Christ paid for our redemption (Luke 22:19; 1 Corinthians 11:24–25). Whenever we partake of the bread and the cup, we affirm that Christ has been sacrificed as our Passover lamb (1 Corinthians 5:7). We celebrate the fact that we are one with Christ and enjoy "communion" with Him.

But there is another side to our observance of the Lord's Supper. It is as much a reminder of the bond we share with other believers as it is a reminder of our union with Christ. "The whole Christian world is a passover company gathered around the paschal lamb, and by their participation in it exhibiting their essential unity" wrote theologian B. B. Warfield. "When we bless the cup of blessing, it is communion in the blood of Christ; when we break the loaf, it is communion in the body of Christ; and because it is one loaf, however many we are, we are one body, as all sharing from one loaf."[13] That is why the celebration of the Lord's Supper is also a time to engage in self-examination and remove any spiritual barriers that separate us from God or other believers (1 Corinthians 11:28).

4. Prayer

The fourth foundational discipline mentioned in Acts 2:42 is prayer. Saying that prayer is one of the means that God uses to promote spiritual growth in the believer is a little like saying that breathing is one of the means used to keep us alive. It is so obvious one might think that it hardly needs to be mentioned. Yet few believers are really satisfied with their prayer life. Perhaps this is because we feel that something so necessary must be easy. Prayer, however, does not always come automatically or easily, even to those who know its importance.

Disciplined prayer is work and requires a measure of preparation. The first step is to find a place with relatively few distractions. Second, expect to have to deal with wandering thoughts. We should not be discouraged when they come but simply acknowledge their presence and redirect our mind to God. Third, our prayers ought to be fueled by a sense of our own need and rooted in our confidence that the prayer of the righteous is powerful and effective (James 5:16).

John Calvin divided prayer into two basic types. First are seasons of prayer when, using our troubles, discomforts, fears, and trials, "God pricks us the more sharply, as occasion demands, to pray earnestly."[14] The other type of prayer is disciplined prayer "at all times" (cf. Ephesians 6:18; 1 Thessalonians 5:17). Both are important, but Calvin viewed the second type of prayer as more important because we need God as much in times of prosperity as we do in times of trouble but are less likely to remember Him.

It's About Relationship

Fortunately, we do not need to be able to practice the spiritual disciplines perfectly before we can get any benefit from them. We do need to take care, however, that they do not become an end in themselves.

The history of the church demonstrates that the use of "spiritual exercises" often degenerates into a works-based approach to the Christian life. When the disciplines are removed from the context of grace and divine empowerment, they become spiritually toxic. Practicing the disciplines helps to prepare for the challenges of discipleship. They are not themselves the essence of discipleship. Being a disciple is first and foremost a matter of relationship.

CHRISTIAN
VIRTUES

THE MARKS OF
SPIRITUAL MATURITY

I am not the man I once was. My hair is thinner, my eyes are weaker, and my waistline is larger. If I haven't reached it already, I am swiftly approaching the stage in life that is usually described by the euphemistic term "mature." It is not a popular adjective. If my wife were to try on a new dress and ask for my opinion, she would not be pleased if I were to reply, "You look mature." But when it comes to the Christian life, things are different. She would be very happy if I were to tell her that she was a mature Christian.

Spiritual maturity is the goal of every serious disciple of Christ. But what standard should we use to measure it? In the natural realm there are objective standards that can be used to measure a person's growth and development. When my children were small, the doctor would measure their weight and height and check their reflexes to make sure that they were developing correctly.

The Bible has its own way of measuring the spiritual life of the believer. According to Ephesians 4:13, God's ultimate goal for the Christian is to "become mature," which is further defined as "the whole measure of the fullness of Christ." This is what we will look like at the end of our redemptive experience. We will be like Christ. As John wrote, "Now we are children of God, and what we will be has not yet been made known. But we know that when he appears, we shall be like him, for we shall see him as he is" (1 John 3:2).

When we ask ourselves what spiritual maturity looks like, the answer is that Christ Himself is the standard.

But is it really possible to measure our progress toward spiritual maturity? Are there objective markers with which we can measure ourselves? When our pediatrician wanted to know how well my sons were growing, he would compare their development to a chart that listed national standards based on other children their age. The New Testament doesn't provide us with a "chart," but it does contain several lists that give us a snapshot of what our spiritual growth should look like. One of the most foundational is contained in the Sermon on the Mount. It is the list of characteristics known as the Beatitudes (Matthew 5:1–11). It is certainly the most famous and probably one of the most misunderstood sections of Scripture in the Bible.

Many people regard the Beatitudes to be the essence of all that Jesus taught and view these sayings as preconditions to eternal life. The reverse is actually the truth. The characteristics described in the Beatitudes are the marks of those who already know Christ. This is because they describe characteristics that must be produced in the believer by the Holy Spirit.

The Beatitudes do not give us a picture of human morality; they are a picture of spiritual transformation. D. Martyn Lloyd-Jones explained, "None of these descriptions refers to what we may call a natural tendency. Each one of them is wholly a disposition which is produced by grace alone and the operation of the Holy Spirit upon us."[1]

LOSING OUR LIVES FOR CHRIST

The point made by Lloyd-Jones is evident to anyone who has seriously studied Jesus' list. Indeed, from a human perspective, many of these characteristics seem paradoxical. Humanly speaking, they are the opposite of what we would expect. One important lesson in this is that we don't always know what is good for us. Following our natural inclinations may move us further away from spiritual maturity rather than closer to it.

The Beatitudes also reveal the danger of approaching the Christian life as a consumer, picking out the aspects of it that we like and ignoring those elements that make us uncomfortable. We like the promises of forgiveness and salvation but don't want to be troubled by Christ's lordship or His call to obedience. We are drawn to the blessings of righteousness but are not attracted by the corresponding warnings that there is also a measure of loss involved in following Christ.

Jesus Himself said, "If anyone would come after me, he must deny himself and take up his cross and follow me. For whoever wants to save his life will lose it, but whoever loses his life for me will find it. What good will it be for a man if he gains the whole world, yet forfeits his soul? Or what can a man give in exchange for his soul?" (Matthew 16:24–26). It should come as no surprise, then, that the first four traits that Jesus describes in the Beatitudes are negative in nature. They promise blessedness to those who are aware of their own spiritual poverty, mourn over sin, refuse to cling to their rights, and hunger for righteousness (Matthew 5:3–6).

Some time ago I watched video footage on television of a group that had gone white-water rafting on a particularly dangerous stretch of river. The raft came to a spot in the river known as a "hole," where a powerful whirlpool threatened to spin and spill the craft. Sure enough, the craft overturned, and everyone inside was sucked down by the current. One woman clung tightly to the raft, desperately trying to keep her head above water. What she did not realize was that by doing so she was also in danger of being dragged underneath the raft by the current and smothered by the very thing she hoped would save her. Her friends, who had let go of the raft and made their way to the security of a nearby rock, pleaded with her to let go and let the current and her life jacket do their work. At first she was unwilling to do so. After what must have seemed like an eternity, she finally did release her grip and disappeared under the water. A few moments later she popped up farther down the river and was pulled to safety.

In the same way, the transformation Jesus described in the first four Beatitudes calls us to release our grip on self-life and abandon ourselves to the current of His love and the transforming, lifting power of His Spirit. In the process, we disappear as we are changed into the likeness of Christ. The prospect of losing ourselves is not a comfortable one. Yet every loss implied in the Beatitudes is coupled with a corresponding blessing.

WITH LOSS COMES BLESSING

Those who recognize their poverty of spirit, for example, know that the only way to obtain the kingdom of heaven is to receive it as a gift. Being poor in spirit begins when we declare spiritual bankruptcy and turn to Christ. But it also demands that we turn the management of our lives over to Christ. When Christ enters the believer's life, He brings with Him an entirely new system of accounting. Paul described what this looked like in his own experience when he said that he reckoned all that he had formerly regarded profitable to be loss for the sake of Christ (Philippians 3:8).

In a similar paradox, Jesus promised that those who mourn over their sin would find comfort. They discover what Jesus meant when He said that He did not come to call the righteous but sinners (Mark 2:17). This connection between mourning and comfort sounds odd to us because we believe that comfort ought to be the goal, not mourning. In cases of ordinary grief, comfort is given in the hope that it will alleviate and perhaps even eradicate mourning. In the life of the spirit, however, mourning is desirable because it leads to comfort. This is because Jesus is talking about a very specific kind of mourning. It is mourning over sin.

This recognition of my spiritual poverty causes me to grieve over my sinfulness, and in turn it produces within me humility that is reflected in the next Beatitude—a spirit of meekness. Our culture regards meekness as a character flaw. A meek person is considered a "wimp"—

someone with little backbone. Because of this, while Jesus' promise that the meek will "inherit the earth" has a poetic ring to it, it holds little appeal for the modern ear. We don't want to be meek. We want to be "dynamic." We want to be "powerful." We want to be "in control."

There is power in meekness, but it is a very special kind of power. It is the power to deal with others gently. Some versions actually translate this Beatitude "Blessed are the gentle" (note, for instance, the New American Standard Bible). Gentleness is a form of strength because it requires self-control. The author of the book of Proverbs confirms this when he says, "Better a patient man than a warrior, a man who controls his temper than one who takes a city" (Proverbs 16:32). Meekness also expresses itself in obedience. Where our relationship with God is concerned, meekness is not a matter of cowering and whispering in His presence. It is an attitude of responsiveness that is eager to say yes to God. Those who are meek receive God's Word with humility (James 1:21).

The power of meekness is proven further by the example of those who are described as "meek" in the Bible. Moses, Jesus, and Paul are all characterized as meek or gentle (Numbers 12:3; Matthew 11:29; 1 Corinthians 4:21; 2 Corinthians 10:1).

These three negative characteristics combine to produce a very positive result in the disciple. They create an intense desire or "hunger" for righteousness.

THE HUNGER THAT HEALS THE SOUL

My mother grew up during the era of the Great Depression. At times her family had so little food that they would go for days without eating. She often spoke of times when all the family had to eat was a can of beans. When my father began dating her and brought her to his parents' home for dinner, she would eat ravenously, as if she never expected to see food again. That kind of experience is alien to me. The only time I have ever missed a meal is when I was trying to lose weight. But in Jesus' day, hunger was a common experience. There were no government programs to provide a safety net for the poor. The Law of Moses did make provision for the poor by commanding farmers to leave the corners of their fields unharvested so that the poor could gather the leavings that were dropped there, but the poor were only entitled to what they were able to gather by hand. This meant that a poor Israelite wouldn't starve but would face a daily search for food. Satisfying one's hunger was a constant challenge, and the only real hope was in God's gracious provision.

Imagine, then, how strange Jesus' words must have seemed to those who were wondering where they were going to find that evening's meal: "Blessed are those who hunger and thirst for righteousness (Matthew 5:6)." This beatitude implies that spiritual hunger and thirst are evidence of an even deeper need than their physical counterparts. They make us aware of what we lack and force us to acknowledge a longing for that which only Christ can supply.

This kind of hunger and thirst is desperately needed today. There are many like those in the church of Laodicea, of whom Christ declared, "You say, 'I am rich; I have acquired wealth and do not need a thing.' But you do not realize that you are wretched, pitiful, poor, blind and naked" (Revelation 3:17). Spiritual hunger is a hunger that heals. It opens our eyes to see our true need and weans us from lesser things that cannot ultimately satisfy us.

MERCY, PURITY, AND PEACE

The next three beatitudes are essentially positive and reflect God's own character: "Blessed are the merciful . . . the pure in heart . . . the peacemakers" (Matthew 5:7–9). The qualities of mercy, purity of heart, and peacemaking are all reflections of divine attributes and behavior. God is gracious and compassionate and calls His people to exercise compassion toward others (Exodus 22:27). He shows mercy (Exodus 33:19). He is a holy God who calls His people to be holy (Leviticus 11:44–45).

The priority of holiness was vividly portrayed in the Law of Moses through its repeated emphasis on ritual purity. In the sixth beatitude, however, Jesus reveals that the root of true holiness is ultimately a matter of the heart. When we speak, our words reflect the status of the heart (Matthew 12:34; cf. Matthew 15:11). The heart is the root of all behavior, whether it is good or evil: "For out of the heart come evil thoughts, murder, adultery, sexual immorality, theft, false testimony, slander" (Matthew 15:19; cf. Luke 6:45).

Peacemaking, although it is an action, is also a reflection of the character of God. God is the source of peace for His people (Psalm 4:8; 29:11). It was the Father's good pleasure to reconcile us through Christ "by making peace through his blood, shed on the cross"(Colossians 1:20). As ambassadors for Christ, we join the Father in this same activity by imploring others to be reconciled to God through Christ (2 Corinthians 5:20).

WHEN PERSECUTION COMES

Although the final beatitude promises a blessing to those who are persecuted for Christ's sake, it implies that those who experience such persecution reflect Christ's righteousness. They are persecuted "because of righteousness" (Matthew 5:10). The apostle Paul warns, "Everyone who wants to live a godly life in Christ Jesus will be persecuted" (2 Timothy 3:12). These warnings are not given to encourage us to seek persecution but to let us know that it will be an unavoidable reality if we live a godly life.

However, if people speak poorly of us, we should not automatically assume that we are suffering for the sake of righteousness. If people say that we are narrow-minded, opinionated, judgmental, and obnoxious, perhaps the real problem is that we are narrow minded, opinionated, judgmental, and obnoxious. It may have nothing to do with Christ at all. If I think that I am experiencing "persecution" from coworkers, friends, or family members, the first thing I ought to ask is whether I have brought any of it on myself. Is it possible that I believe the right things but am living my life in the wrong way?

The apostle Peter warns that there is no credit in suffering for doing wrong. It is suffering for the sake of doing right that God finds commendable (1 Peter 2:20).

The blessedness of persecution is not in the experience of suffering but in what that persecution implies about us. If it is genuinely persecution for the sake of righteousness, it means that those who are persecuting us have seen the reflection of Christ in our lives.

Jesus warned His disciples that they would be hated because of Him and be persecuted from one city to another during their lifetime (Matthew 10:21–23). Jesus also encouraged them with the reminder that they were only experiencing the same kind of treatment that He Himself had suffered. "A student is not above his teacher, nor a servant above his master. It is enough for the student to be like his teacher, and the servant like his master. If the head of the house has been called Beelzebub, how much more the members of his household!" (Matthew 10:24–25).

PRODUCING SPIRITUAL FRUIT

The Beatitudes pronounce a blessing on those who exhibit foundational spiritual characteristics but they do not say directly how those characteristics are developed. Paul's list in Galatians 5:22–23, on the other hand, roots the believer's character in the work of the Holy Spirit. Paul calls the following "the fruit of the Spirit": love, joy, peace, patience, kindness, goodness, faithfulness, gentleness, and self-control. The fact that he refers to them as spiritual "fruit" contrasts them with the acts (literally "works") of the sinful nature described in the preceding verses (Galatians 5:19–21). This difference in language underscores a fundamental difference in their origin. The acts of the flesh are self-generated. They are the natural result of the sinful nature.

The characteristics that Paul has described as the fruit of the Spirit, on the other hand, have a supernatural origin. The Holy Spirit produces them. These characteristics can be divided into clusters of three.

Fruit of Our Inner Disposition

The first cluster, consisting of love, joy, and peace, do not describe a specific behavior but speak of the believer's inner disposition. Elsewhere, Paul linked love, joy, and peace with the ministry of the Holy

Spirit to the believer. For example, in Romans 5:5 he wrote, "God has poured out his love into our hearts by the Holy Spirit, whom he has given us." It is not so much the believer's ability to love others that Paul had in mind here, but the believer's subjective experience of God's love. Likewise, in Romans 14:17 he said that "the kingdom of God is not a matter of eating and drinking, but of righteousness, peace and joy in the Holy Spirit." In Romans 15:13 he prayed, "May the God of hope fill you with all joy and peace as you trust in him, so that you may overflow with hope by the power of the Holy Spirit."

Love, joy, and peace are linked together in Romans 5 but in a different order. Peace is mentioned first, followed by joy in Romans 5:1–2: "Therefore, since we have been justified through faith, we have peace with God through our Lord Jesus Christ, through whom we have gained access by faith into this grace in which we now stand. And we rejoice in the hope of the glory of God." The peace that is mentioned in Romans 5:1 is positional in nature. It is peace "with God." In this case Paul was not referring to the subjective experience of peace, but to the new position that the believer experiences in relation to God as a result of having been justified by faith. This objective condition of being at peace produces the subjective experience of joy. Because we are no longer God's enemies, we can rejoice in the hope of the glory of God.

This is rejoicing that is sparked by our anticipation of the future, but it also has a very practical result in the present. It enables the believer to rejoice in suffering. "Not only so, but we also rejoice in our sufferings," Paul wrote, "because we know that suffering produces perseverance; perseverance, character; and character, hope" (Romans 5:3–4). Paul was not saying here that being at peace with God makes suffering enjoyable. The believer's ability to rejoice in suffering is grounded in the knowledge that God is using the experience to transform our character. It produces perseverance, character, and hope.

Fruits with an Outward Focus

The next triad in Galatians 5:22–23 is made up of characteristics that have an outward focus. They are patience, kindness, and goodness.

All three are characteristics of God. He is patient because He is "the compassionate and gracious God, slow to anger, abounding in love and faithfulness, maintaining love to thousands, and forgiving wickedness, rebellion and sin" (Exodus 34:6–7a). God's patience is not limited to His own people. He is patient with believers and unbelievers alike. This does not mean, however, that He ignores sin. The psalmist declares: "God is a righteous judge, a God who expresses his wrath every day" (Psalm 7:11). Because of this, God's wrath is to be feared (Psalm 76:7). Yet instead of exercising His anger over sin in judgment, God shows patience on a daily basis to those who deserve His wrath. He does this in order to give them an opportunity to come to repentance and faith in Christ (2 Peter 3:9).

The apostle Paul saw himself as the supreme example of this. Prior to his conversion he was a blasphemer and persecutor of the church. Yet this was also the reason he was shown mercy, so that "Christ Jesus might display his unlimited patience as an example for those who would believe on him and receive eternal life" (1 Timothy 1:16).

Those who have experienced God's patience have an obligation to show patience to others. In practical terms, this is carried out by "bearing with one another in love" (Ephesians 4:2). Since the church is made up of those who are in a variety of stages in their spiritual growth, there will be plenty of opportunities for aggravation, hurt, and mutual disappointment among believers. There is a sense in which we have been called to "put up with one another" in the body of Christ. This is to be done in an attitude of love rather than in a condescending manner. However, since we are self-centered by nature, it must also be done in the power of the Holy Spirit.

Patience is essentially a passive quality. It refrains from taking action. Kindness is its active counterpart. Kindness is demonstrated to others.

God's kindness is not limited to believers. He shows kindness even to those who do not appreciate it and to those who do not deserve it (Luke 6:35). His ultimate act of kindness was in showing grace to us through His Son, Jesus Christ (Ephesians 2:7; Titus 3:4). In Romans 2:4, Paul linked God's kindness with tolerance and patience and noted that the purpose of God's kindness is to lead us to repentance. As with patience, those who have experienced God's kindness have an obligation to show kindness to others. A disposition of kindness motivates us to meet the needs of others.

Goodness, the third companion in this triad, is what kindness looks like in action. It involves more than simply being good; it is reflected in the believer's life by doing good to others. New Testament scholar F. F. Bruce noted that in Paul's lists of the works of the flesh and the fruit of the Spirit, goodness is the alternative to envy. The spiritual fruit of goodness is demonstrated in a generous spirit.[2]

Certainly, we show generosity in the way we handle our finances. But it is not limited to this realm. The spiritual fruit of goodness is the same attitude of humility described in Philippians 2:3–4: "Do nothing out of selfish ambition or vain conceit, but in humility consider others better than yourselves. Each of you should look not only to your own interests, but also to the interests of others." Those who possess the fruit of goodness show a sympathetic interest in others and are as concerned about their well-being and advancement as they are about their own.

Fruit of a Spirit-Controlled Self-Mastery

The third triad in Galatians 5:22–23 lists characteristics that show evidence of Spirit-controlled self-mastery. The first of these, translated "faithfulness," is actually the word "faith" in the Greek text. The context, however, suggests that in this case Paul is not thinking of faith in God but of reliable or dependable character on the part of the believer. This is the characteristic of Spirit-enabled consistency.

Like the other characteristics in this list, faithfulness is an attribute of God. God demonstrates His faithfulness by keeping His promises and by acting justly (Deuteronomy 7:9; 32:4). His actions are always consistent with what He has revealed about Himself in His Word; "he is faithful in all he does" (Psalm 33:4).

We live in an age when talk is cheap and promises are as easily broken as they are made. We have come to expect loopholes and escape clauses in the most important commitments. Yet Jesus told His disciples, "Simply let your 'Yes' be 'Yes' and your 'No,' 'No'; anything beyond this comes from the evil one" (Matthew 5:37).

The common practice of making casual vows to God prompted Christ's command. In Old Testament worship a vow was a voluntary commitment made by the believer to God. It might be a commitment to abstain from doing something or it could involve a promise to take an action or make an offering. Ecclesiastes 5:4–7 warned Old Testament worshipers to think carefully before making a vow to God and urged them not to delay when fulfilling it. "It is better not to vow," the author wrote, "than to make a vow and not fulfill it" (Ecclesiastes 5:5).

But in Jesus' day vows were used mostly as a figure of speech. The rabbis had devised an elaborate system of oaths in which some were binding and some were not. They considered an oath sworn by heaven, for example, to be more binding than an oath sworn by earth. An oath sworn by the city of Jerusalem was not binding unless one happened to be facing Jerusalem at the time. The practical result of this system was that these promises actually became a sophisticated form of lying.

Jesus called His disciples to a simple rule of speaking the truth. Those who are faithful in speech keep their commitments, whether they have been made to God or to man. They "speak the truth in love" (Ephesians 4:15). This also means that they take the other person's need into account before they speak. Thus Paul warns believers, "Let your conversation be always full of grace, seasoned with salt, so that you may know how to answer everyone" (Colossians 4:6).

God also demonstrates His faithfulness by carrying on to completion the work of sanctification that He has begun in us through Christ (1 Thessalonians 5:23–24). We do not have to worry that He will grow tired of us and give up. God's faithfulness is not contingent on our performance. Even though we are unfaithful to Him at times, He is always faithful to us (2 Timothy 2:13).

Since God has shown this kind of loyalty to us, we have an obligation to show it to others. We are to accept one another the way that Christ has accepted us (Romans 15:7). This kind of faithfulness is anchored in love, which is not self-seeking, is not easily angered, and does not keep a record of wrongs. It does not enjoy hearing an account of the evil that others have done but rejoices in the truth. It is quick to protect the interests of others and prefers to expect the best from them (1 Corinthians 13:5–7).

If faithfulness is expressed in loyalty toward others, it should be no surprise that Paul associates faithfulness with the fruit of gentleness. Loyalty prompts us to be committed to dealing truthfully with others. Gentleness enables us to be considerate in the way that we relate to them. Gentleness is one of the characteristics of Christ (Matthew 11:29). It is rooted in the foundational Beatitude of meekness (Matthew 5:5). Gentleness does not come to us automatically. We must choose the path of gentleness when dealing with others. In Colossians 3:12 we are told to "clothe" ourselves with gentleness. It is an especially important trait when dealing with others who are caught in sin (Galatians 6:1).

The Puritan writer Thomas Watson compared this responsibility of dealing gently with the fallen to the work of a surgeon: "If a bone be out of joint, the surgeon must not use a rough hand that may chance break another bone. But he must come gently to the work, and afterwards bind it up softly."[3] This is certainly beneficial to the one who needs to be restored. But it is also in the best interest of the one who does the restoring. Dealing gently with those who have fallen and are repentant is really a matter of treating others the way we ourselves would want to be treated.

The last fruit of the Spirit mentioned in Paul's list in Galatians 5:22–23 is self-control. Its opposites among the works of the flesh are sexual immorality, impurity, and debauchery (Galatians 5:19). The battleground in the practice of self-control is within the individual, but the victory is corporate in nature because those who fail to practice self-control cannot help but victimize others when they indulge in such works.

The Scriptures make it clear that the alternative to a life governed by self-control is bondage. In Romans 6:16, Paul asks, "Don't you know that when you offer yourselves to someone to obey him as slaves, you are slaves to the one whom you obey—whether you are slaves to sin, which leads to death, or to obedience, which leads to righteousness?" Likewise, Peter warns that a man is a slave to whatever has mastered him (2 Peter 2:19).

The fruit of self-control is much more than the decision to "just say no." It is a daily, and even moment-by-moment application of the Cross to our affections, thoughts, and actions. Every time we exercise self-control we declare with our lives the gospel truth that "those who belong to Christ Jesus have crucified the sinful nature with its passions and desires" (Galatians 5:24). Ultimately, this is what it means to walk in the Spirit.

If I am not the man I once was, it is also true that I am not yet the person that I will be. Through the finished work of Christ and the ongoing ministry of the Holy Spirit, God is doing a work of transformation in my life. He is laying a foundation of spiritual characteristics like those described in the Beatitudes and adding to that foundation the fruit of the Spirit. The finished work will be a living and eternal monument to His grace. This is not just true of me. It is the case with everyone who is a disciple of Jesus Christ.

THE SPIRITUAL
JOURNEY

GOD'S PATTERN
OF TRAINING

At some point on every vacation trip our family has ever taken, my boys have asked the one question that has been on the lips of children since travel began: "Are we almost there yet?" My wife's reply is always the same. "We're closer than we've ever been!"

I can remember asking the same question on long road trips to visit my uncles and aunts. No matter how long we had been traveling, my parents' reply, like that of my wife, always seemed to be the same: "Not yet."

As I got older, I learned to look for landmarks along the way. When the neat rows of suburban homes gave way to farmers' fields, I knew we were finally leaving the "city" and were now in the "country." We weren't close, however, until I saw the old weathered barn with the Mail Pouch Tobacco sign painted on its broad side. When that came into view, I knew that it wouldn't be long before I saw the two stone pillars, each with the painted profile of an Indian, that told me we were about to turn onto my favorite uncle's street.

The spiritual life is also a journey, and like every journey, it has its own distinct landmarks.

CALLED TO FOLLOW CHRIST

The Fisherman and the Carpenter

Consider Simon, a bleary eyed fisherman, sore after a fruitless night of casting the net. He and his companions wearily rinse out their fishnets in the shallow water of the lake and hang them over the crossbar of the ship's mast to dry. Simon shields his eyes from the sun as he scans the shoreline and spots a crowd beginning to converge farther down the beach. The voice that rises above its growing murmur is a familiar one to him.

So is the figure at its center, drawing the multitude to Him as if He were a magnet and they were shards of iron. It is Jesus of Nazareth. When the eager crowd looks like it is about to push Him into the lake, Jesus signals Simon and asks to use one of the boats as a pulpit. Simon agrees. The nets are quickly taken down and stowed, and the boat is launched back into the water.

When Jesus finishes His teaching from the boat, Simon and his small crew are left to contemplate the steady lapping of the water against the hull, the sound of the departing crowd, and the occasional cry of a gull high over head. Simon is about to tell the men to return to shore when Jesus speaks again. This time it isn't a request. It's a command. Jesus fixes His gaze on Simon and says, "Move the ship out into deep water." Then Jesus turns to the ship's crew and says, "Let down the nets for a catch."

With eyebrows raised, the crew looks from Simon to Jesus and then back to Simon again. They are wondering if this is a joke. After all, this carpenter turned itinerant rabbi has just told them to do the wrong thing at the wrong time. Night is the proper time to catch fish, and they have just spent an entire night catching nothing. But Jesus' gaze is unflinching.

After an uncomfortable moment of silence, Simon finally speaks. "Master, we've worked hard all night and haven't caught anything. But because you say so, I will let down the nets." There is a hint of patient condescension in Simon's voice. After all, what does a carpenter-turned-clergyman have to say to a fisherman about catching fish? Quite a bit, actually, if that carpenter also happens to be the Creator of the universe! But Simon doesn't know that yet.

With a sigh of resignation and perhaps a blush of embarrassment for Jesus, the men drop the nets. They do it with the ease of those who have performed the same task so many times that they no longer have to think about it. Just as they have done a thousand times before, they watch each net slide into the water and go limp. *No one likes to see a good man proven wrong,* they reason to themselves. *But Jesus asked for it. He should stick to what He knows best and leave us to what we know best.*

Suddenly their weathered hands feel an unmistakable tug. Eyes widen with amazement and recognition. They have done this night after night for months on end, but the nets never felt like this! It is the unmistakable feel of a catch. But what a catch! One net writhes as if it is a living thing. It is so full, it is in danger of bursting. There are so many fish that the men can't even haul the net into the boat.

Now they are laughing and shouting. Someone is signaling to James and John, Simon's partners, to come and help.

A Fisherman's Confession

But not Simon. As the heavy net is dragged aboard, weighing down the boat so much that it begins to sink, Simon stares at Jesus. His smile of patient condescension has turned to wide-eyed amazement. Amazement turns to fear. Tears stream down Simon's face as he falls on his knees.

"Go away from me, Lord!" Simon cries. "I am a sinful man!"

Jesus doesn't disagree. Instead, He offers Simon these words of hope: "Don't be afraid; from now on you will catch men" (Luke 5:8–11). From that point on, Simon, the Galilean fisherman whom Jesus eventually renamed Peter, pulled his boat up on shore and left everything and followed Christ. This was not the first time that he had heard Christ's promise. In fact, it was actually the third time that he had been called to follow Jesus.

STAGES OF COMMITMENT

Simon Peter's commitment to Christ grew in stages. It began when his brother Andrew, a follower of John the Baptist, personally introduced him to Jesus. At that first meeting, Jesus gave Simon a new name. He told him, "You are Simon son of John. You will be called Cephas"(John 1:42). *Cephas* was an Aramaic term that meant "stone" or "rock." *Peter* is its Greek equivalent. This new name was probably intended to picture the transformation Christ would bring about in Peter's life.

A year later Jesus came to Peter and Andrew while they were fishing, called them to follow Him in discipleship, and promised to make them fishers of men (Matthew 4:18–22; cf. Mark 1:16–20). Not long after this, Christ repeated this promise to Peter, after the miraculous catch of fish described in Luke 5:1–11.

After Peter denied Christ, Jesus appeared to him following the Resurrection and commissioned him again, saying, "Feed my sheep" (John 21:15–17).

Although we have not been called to be apostles like Peter was, there are many parallels between his experience and our own. For example, God probably used some other person to introduce us to Christ, as He used Andrew to introduce Peter. It may have been a parent, relative, friend, or coworker. Or we may have learned about Christ through the preaching of a pastor or the instruction of a Sunday school teacher.

Also, like Peter, our call to discipleship may have come in stages and may have been reinforced by Christ more than once. For some of us, this was because we did not make a serious commitment to living for Christ in our daily life when we accepted Him as Savior. Ideally, those who acknowledge Christ as their Savior also commit themselves to following Jesus as Lord. In some cases, however, full commitment comes later, often due to lack of teaching. Others, who do make a serious commitment to following Christ, are called like Peter to serve Him in new ways.

WHO CAN BE A DISCIPLE?

But what kind of person is best suited to be a disciple?

Extraordinary Risk Takers . . .

Early in the twentieth century, South Pole explorer Sir Ernest Shackleton attempted to cross Antarctica. Before he had completed the journey, however, his ship, the *Endurance,* became trapped in the ice fields of the Weddell Sea. Shackleton and his crew hoped to wait until the spring thaw to continue their expedition, but the ice that had hemmed them in also crushed their vessel. Shackleton and the twenty-seven survivors took dog sleds and several small boats and made their way across moving ice floes to the safety of Elephant Island. Once there, he left all but five of the crew behind and crossed the Scotia Sea in an open boat, an eight hundred-mile voyage across some of the most dangerous waters on the planet, until they landed on the southern coast of South Georgia Island.

However, Shackleton's ordeal was still not over. Shackleton left three of the remaining crew on the coast, while he and two companions crossed the mountains on foot until they arrived at the Stromness whaling station on the other side of South Georgia. Shackleton later returned to rescue all twenty-two of the men that had been left on Elephant Island and the three that had been left on the South Georgian coast.[1]

Before this ill-fated expedition had begun, Shackleton had placed an ad in a London newspaper that read: "Men wanted for hazardous journey. Small wages, bitter cold, long months of complete darkness, constant danger, safe return doubtful." He had expected few to inquire. Instead, so many had applied that most had to be turned away.

"It seemed as though all the men in Great Britain were determined to accompany us," Shackleton later observed.[2]

. . . or Ordinary Men and Women?

I would not have been one of them. I would like to think that I might have responded to Shackleton's ad, but I know myself too well. I am not a thrill seeker. I don't hunger for new experiences. When I go to the restaurant, I want to order something I have tried before. The last time I rode on a roller coaster, I closed my eyes during the entire ride and prayed for it to end. I like my adventure in a novel. As much as I would like to believe that I am "hero" material, I know that I am just an ordinary person.

The good news is that Christ calls ordinary people to be His disciples. The disciples we read about in the Bible were not superhuman. They were people like Elijah, "a man just like us" (James 5:17). They were ordinary people who took God at His word and were used by Him in extraordinary ways.

Christ's disciples were "unschooled, ordinary men" (Acts 4:13). Unlike the scribes who were trained scholars, they were simply "laymen" who had spent time with Christ.

Peter: Willing to Listen and Learn

Peter, in particular, was given to hasty judgments and rash commitments (Matthew 16:22–23; 26:33–35). He had a tendency to speak and act without thinking (Mark 9:5–6; John 18:10). Bold in his faith one minute, he sank beneath the waves of doubt and fear the next (Matthew 14:25–31; 26:69–75). Peter's character changed radically after the Day of Pentecost. The man who had been so afraid of losing his life that he had denied Christ when challenged by a mere servant, boldly proclaimed Him, often to the same rulers that had arranged the crucifixion (Acts 2:14–40; 3:12–26; 4:1–22; 5:17–42). Yet even then, Peter still had important lessons to learn. On one occasion he had to be publicly rebuked by Paul for hypocritically refusing to eat with Gentile believers (Galatians 2:11–14).

Peter grew in His understanding of what it meant to follow Christ by listening to Jesus teach. When Peter tried to persuade Jesus not to go to Jerusalem, Jesus taught him about the necessity of taking up the cross (Matthew 16:21–24). When Peter fell asleep in the garden, Jesus taught him that it was important to "watch and pray" (Mark 14:37–38). Peter often asked Jesus to explain His teachings (Matthew 15:15; Luke 12:41; John 13:36–37). Later in his ministry, Peter would urge other believers to "crave pure spiritual milk" in order to grow (1 Peter 2:2). Peter also learned by doing. Jesus sent the disciples out on ministry assignments (Matthew 10:5; Mark 6:7).

BUMPS IN THE ROAD

Avoiding What Slows You Down

The path toward spiritual maturity is not an easy one. It requires preparation and determination. The author of the book of Hebrews compares it to a race that is so demanding that the runner must remove anything that might be a hindrance: "Therefore, since we are surrounded by such a great cloud of witnesses, let us throw off everything that hinders and the sin that so easily entangles, and let us run with perseverance the race marked out for us" (Hebrews 12:1). In the race of discipleship, we are to remove anything that weighs us down.

In these verses the writer refers to the custom of Greek athletes who stripped down before running a race. His point is an obvious one. If you really want to win a race, anything that slows you down is a liability.

Friends of ours have a son who is on the high school track team. We had them over for dinner one evening, and I offered him some soda pop. I was surprised when he turned me down and asked for water instead. "Don't you like soda pop?" I asked. "Oh, I like it. It's just that I have to run in a race tomorrow." When I was puzzled by his explanation, he told me that the same ingredient that gives soda pop its fizz depletes a runner's oxygen. Normally he would have enjoyed drinking soda pop. But because he wanted to do well in the race, he turned it down.

Following in the Winner's Footsteps

The amazing thing about the Christian life is that it is a race that has already been won. In Hebrews 12:2 runners in the Christian race are urged to fix their eyes on Jesus who is described as "the author and perfecter of our faith." The Greek term that is translated "author" referred to a leader or pioneer. The term "perfecter" refers to one who completes something. Jesus is the starter in the race of faith. He is also the finisher. But notice what it is He finishes. It is faith—my faith. As we cope with the struggle of running the race of the Christian life, we have the comfort of following in the footsteps of someone who has blazed the trail before us.

Jesus has already run the race, and He has completed the course. In most races the victory only comes to the one who is the first to cross the finish line. In the race of the Christian life, every believer's victory is assured because someone else has already been declared the winner. When Jesus ran the race, He wasn't running for Himself. He was running for me. When He lived a perfect life, He lived it for me. When He died a sacrificial death on the cross, He died for me. He rose in victory and is seated at the right hand of the Father in heaven, where He prays for me. The life that I now live, no matter how difficult the struggle, is really just a victory lap.

The Not-Always-Comfortable Journey

Christ's death and resurrection assure me that victory is guaranteed, but they don't necessarily guarantee me a comfortable journey. In fact, Hebrews 12:2–4 implies that a certain amount of discomfort is inevitable in the Christian life: "Consider him who endured such opposition from sinful men, so that you will not grow weary and lose heart. In your struggle against sin, you have not yet resisted to the point of shedding your blood."

Those words are even more amazing when we consider all that his original readers had suffered. According to Hebrews 10:32–34, they had been publicly insulted, persecuted, and had even had their property confiscated. At that time they had accepted all these things joyfully because of their conviction that something better was waiting for them at the end of their journey. By the time this letter was written, however, some of them had begun to falter. They had been doing their best to run the race of the Christian life, but it had been even harder than they had expected.

In effect, the author of Hebrews tells them, "Don't give up now. Tough it out!"

SPECIAL TRAINING

Accepting Hardship

God often uses hardship to help us grow. The author of Hebrews referred to this as "discipline" in Hebrews 12:7. However, this is a very special kind of discipline. In view of the "race" analogy of the previous verses, we might have expected him to use an athletic term. Instead, he used a term that refers to parental training.

Often when hardship enters our lives it is God's way of exercising parental discipline. In Hebrews 12:5–6, the author of the book of Hebrews warns us to avoid two possible reactions to this experience. Citing Proverbs 3:11–12, he warns us not to treat God's correction with contempt by making light of the Lord's discipline. Today he might say, "Don't blow it off."

The other danger is the temptation to become discouraged or "lose heart." Like the teenager who becomes so frustrated with her parents that she storms into the bedroom and slams the door, we can become angry at the way God has arranged the circumstances of our lives. We slam the door of our hearts and echo the complaint of the old saint who prayed, "Lord, if this is the way you treat your friends, no wonder you have so few of them!" But is it realistic for God to expect us to get excited about divine discipline? Nobody enjoys discomfort, at least nobody normal.

Divine Discipline: A Sign of Love

The secret to enduring divine discipline is to look at it through the eyes of God and interpret its message: It is a sign of His love. "Endure hardship as discipline; God is treating you as sons. For what son is not disciplined by his father? If you are not disciplined (and everyone undergoes discipline), then you are illegitimate children and not true sons" (Hebrews 12:7–8).

Discipline tells us something about the nature of God. It tells me that He is a God of love. He is a God who loves us enough to intervene in our lives to the point where it hurts. Divine discipline also tells us something important about ourselves. It says that God has accepted us as His children. The fact that He disciplines us indicates that He has accepted us as His own.

Nearly every time I visit the grocery store, I see a child behaving badly. Sometimes he is demanding that his mom or dad buy him the latest sugar-blasted cereal or a new toy. At other times a child is pushing the shopping cart too fast and bumping into other customers. She may even be throwing a full-blown tantrum in the center of the aisle. Each time my reaction is the same. I walk past that boy or girl. I may shake my head and mutter disapprovingly to my wife, but I won't intervene. Why not? The answer is simple. It isn't my child. The child may need to be disciplined, but that is someone else's responsibility.

This is the point of Hebrews 12:5–8. Divine discipline is a good sign. It is proof that we belong to God. In fact, the analogy between divine discipline and parental training is so strong that the author points to our experience with our own parents to motivate us to be patient (Hebrews 12:9–10). For most of us, discipline isn't a new experience. We have been disciplined by our own parents and have continued to respect them. Why not our heavenly Father?

A Father's Wise Perspective

Not long ago my wife and I were walking through the church parking lot when we noticed a little boy sitting on the curb with his head in his hands and tears streaming down his face. When we asked him what was wrong, he wailed: "He says I can't have it!"

"You can't have what?" I asked.

"A bird. My dad says that I can't have a bird!"

I could tell that at that moment he felt that his father was the meanest person in the world. For a few seconds I wondered if his father wasn't being too strict myself. After all, the boy hadn't asked for something unreasonable. He hadn't asked for a pony or a pet elephant. All he wanted was a tiny bird. But as we talked further, we discovered that his father had said no to his son's request because of allergies. Suddenly, the father's behavior seemed reasonable and loving, at least to me. Interestingly, from the child's point of view, knowing his father's reasoning didn't make him feel any better. He knew why his father had said no, but he was still angry!

A Matter of Trust

The same is often true when it comes to the discipline of our heavenly Father. Knowing why He disciplines us does not necessarily make the experience of discipline more comfortable. "No discipline seems pleasant at the time, but painful," the author of Hebrews observes. "Later on, however, it produces a harvest of righteousness and peace for those who have been trained by it" (Hebrews 12:11).

Ultimately, it is a matter of trust. We are thankful for divine discipline, not because we enjoy it or even because we understand it. We are thankful for it because we know something about the one who administers it. We know that He knows what He is doing better than we do. We know that His purpose for our lives is a good one. Our focus during the process of discipline, then, should not be on the experience itself, but on the outcome that will be produced as a result of God's discipline.

The soldier trains for victory. The musician trains for the thrill of performing. The athlete trains for a trophy. But the Christian undergoes divine discipline for a "harvest of righteousness and peace." God's ultimate objective, according to Hebrews 12:10, is that we may "share in his holiness."

THE VALUE OF HOLINESS

Obviously, in order for this to be of any comfort to us, we must first understand the value of holiness in the Christian life. In his classic book on the subject of holiness, J. C. Ryle observed:

> Suppose for a moment that you were allowed to enter heaven without holiness. What would you do? What possible enjoyment could you feel there? To which of all the saints would you join yourself, and by whose side would you sit down? Their pleasures are not your pleasures, their tastes are not your tastes, their character not your character. How could you possibly be happy, if you had not been holy on earth?[3]

In a similar way, the author of Hebrews emphasizes that God's goal in discipline is to make us holy. God disciplines us so that we may "share in his holiness" (Hebrews 12:10). It "produces a harvest of righteousness" (Hebrews 12:11). Yet when he spells out the implications this has for daily living, he tells us to make every effort to be holy (Hebrews 12:14).

There is no contradiction here. Whether it is the experience of divine discipline or my own grace-empowered effort, God is ultimately the one at work.

Some reasons for experiencing divine discipline are better than others. First Peter 3:17 warns, "It is better, if it is God's will, to suffer for doing good than for doing evil." We do not need to seek suffering; it will find us without our help. Jesus told His disciples that they were genuinely blessed when people insulted, persecuted, and slandered them (Matthew 5:11). He also assured them that persecutions would come (Matthew 24:9). The apostle Paul likewise promised that "everyone who wants to live a godly life in Christ Jesus will be persecuted" (2 Timothy 3:12).

Nowhere, however, are we urged to seek persecution. We are to rejoice in what it says about our Christlikeness, expect it, endure it, and trust in God's power to sustain us through it. We are never told to long for it. Although He may not always answer in the way that we wish, it is always appropriate to ask God to alleviate suffering when it comes (Matthew 26:38–42). It is not always God's will for us to suffer. But when it is, it is better to suffer for the sake of what is right.

One implication of 1 Peter 3:17 is that some forms of suffering may come as a consequence of doing what is wrong. This is true even of some of the suffering we tend to label as persecution. It is important for me, for example, to share my faith with others. But if I am neglecting my job and my employer docks my pay or even fires me, I can't really call that suffering for the sake of righteousness. It may be a form of divine discipline—God may be teaching me a lesson about being a faithful employee. But it would have been better to suffer for doing something right rather than for doing something wrong.

Both the writer of the book of Hebrews and Peter conclude that Jesus is to be our ultimate example when responding to divine discipline. The author of Hebrews urges us to fix our eyes on Jesus, "who for the joy set before him endured the cross, scorning its shame, and sat down at the right hand of the throne of God" (Hebrews 12:2). Similarly, 1 Peter 3:18 sets Christ as the supreme example for those who are called to suffer for the sake of righteousness, noting that His goal was "to bring you to God."

This is both the reward and the inevitable outcome of the journey of faith. We are brought closer to God. We may not have arrived yet. But we are closer than we have ever been.

THE BIBLICAL PATTERN

THE NEW TESTAMENT MODEL OF DISCIPLESHIP

During the nine years that I served as a pastor, discipleship was an important priority in my ministry. I was proud of the fact that I had a "discipleship relationship" with several of the members of my church. In most cases this meant meeting in my home or at the church office for about an hour a week to go over the questions in a small study guide.

The guide contained twelve lessons, each one focusing on a different aspect of the Christian life. Each lesson had questions and Scripture references, space for the user to write a response, and even included cards in the back with verses printed on them that could be used for memorization. It was a complete package. That was one of the reasons I used it.

In time, however, I noticed a disturbing pattern. Although I enjoyed these meetings, they seemed to have relatively little impact on those who attended. Some did grow spiritually as a result of these studies, but nobody turned into the kind of spiritual giant I had hoped to produce. At the end of the twelve weeks, most of the participants seemed to be pretty much the same as when we had started. A few quit attending church during the weeks we went through the booklet, apparently thinking that our discipleship meetings served as a valid substitute. Then when the studies were over, they never came back to church.

After studying what the Bible has to say about this subject, I am convinced that my problem was more a matter of terminology than methodology. What I had been calling "discipleship" was really just a moderately helpful Bible study. For Jesus and the apostles, the practice of discipleship involved much more. They practiced what might be described as "lifestyle discipleship."

THE ORIGINS OF
JESUS' MODEL OF DISCIPLESHIP

Like the Greeks

Jesus did not invent the art of discipleship. A similar practice was already well known among the Greeks and the Jews. Among the Greeks, philosophers like Socrates, Plato, and Aristotle exemplified the practice of instructing disciples. Socrates spent much of his time in public places asking questions and engaging in dialogue. He attracted a group of followers, the most famous of whom was Plato. Like Socrates, Plato also gathered disciples around him and even founded a school. Aristotle was Plato's most famous pupil and engaged in philosophical debate while walking with his students. Those who followed Aristotle's example were called "peripatetic" philosophers, a label based upon the Greek word that means "to walk around."

Like these Greek philosophers, Jesus attracted disciples, engaged in public debate about His teaching, and often used questions in a way that resembled the Socratic method.

Like the Rabbis

Despite these similarities, Jesus' pattern of discipleship was most similar to the practice of the religious leaders of His day. Teachers of the Mosaic Law were known as *scribes* and were commonly addressed as "rabbi." The term *rabbi* comes from a Hebrew word that means "great." In Jesus' day it was synonymous with "teacher" (John 1:38). It was a title of respect used by many to address Jesus and is probably the original term that lies behind the titles of "master" and "Lord" in the Gospels (Luke 5:5, 8). According to the Mishnah, a collection of rabbinical writings that dates back to Jesus' day, this title was used by Jewish students to refer to their teacher. A rabbi's student was known as a *talmid,* a term that comes from the Hebrew verb that meant "to learn." The Mishnah also uses this term to refer to Jesus' disciples. Like the Hebrew term *talmid,* the New Testament word for disciple is also based upon a verb that means "to learn." In simplest terms, then, a disciple is a learner.

The goal of the Jewish *talmid* was to become a rabbi. He devoted himself to the study of Scripture and the memorization of the teaching handed down by the rabbi. Instruction was usually in the form of questions posed by the rabbi and answered by the student. Students addressed the rabbi as "master," "teacher," or sometimes "father," and they were expected to revere him more than their own parents. Students often walked a few feet behind the rabbi. It was not unusual for a rabbi to select one or two students to be his chief disciples. Once the *talmid* achieved the status of rabbi, he attracted his own students and passed on the rabbi's teaching to others.

Jesus followed many of these practices. He frequently used questions as a teaching device. For example, after Jesus' popularity had begun to grow among the multitudes, He took the disciples aside and questioned them about the crowd's opinion of Him (Matthew 16:13). He warned His followers that anyone who did not love Him more than their own mother or father was not fit to be His disciple (Luke 14:26). He expected His disciples to remember His teaching and promised that the coming Holy Spirit would bring it to mind (John 14:23, 26). He expected His disciples to act upon His teaching and told them that the genuineness of their love for Him would be demonstrated by their obedience (John 14:23–24). Jesus even compared the disciples' relationship to Him to that of a slave to his master, saying, "I tell you the truth, no servant is greater than his master, nor is a messenger greater than the one who sent him. Now that you know these things, you will be blessed if you do them" (John 13:16–17).

Those who followed Jesus ministered to His daily needs (Matthew 27:55). At times the disciples literally walked behind Jesus as they traveled from place to place (Mark 10:32). Jesus singled out Peter, James, and John for special attention, allowing them to see and hear things that the other disciples did not (Matthew 17:1; 26:36–37).

SIGNIFICANT DIFFERENCES IN JESUS' APPROACH TO DISCIPLESHIP

The Leader and the Follower as Servants

While it is true that Jesus' pattern of discipleship was influenced by the Jewish concept of the relationship between the rabbi and the *talmid,* He also made some important changes. Jesus allowed others to refer to Him as "rabbi" but commanded His disciples not to use this title. "But you are not to be called 'Rabbi,' for you have only one Master and you are all brothers," He explained. "And do not call anyone on earth 'father,' for you have one Father, and he is in heaven. Nor are you to be called 'teacher,' for you have one Teacher, the Christ" (Matthew 23:8–10). The disciples of Jesus were not to see themselves as "great ones" but as servants (Matthew 23:11).

This was something that Jesus Himself modeled. While a rabbi's disciples often functioned as a kind of personal attendant, Jesus served the disciples. On the night of His betrayal, He performed the task of a common household slave and washed the disciples' feet (John 13:4–5). After His resurrection, He prepared and served a breakfast meal of bread and fish for them (John 21:9–13).

Jesus told the disciples:

> The kings of the Gentiles lord it over them; and those who exercise authority over them call themselves Benefactors. But you are not to be like that. Instead, the greatest among you should be like the youngest, and

the one who rules like the one who serves. For who is greater, the one who is at the table or the one who serves? Is it not the one who is at the table? But I am among you as one who serves." (Luke 22:25–27)

His Authority

Unlike the rabbis of His day, Jesus taught with authority. The teaching of the scribes was heavily dependent upon the tradition of the rabbis that had preceded them. Their instruction often began with the phrase "Rabbi so and so said . . . " Jesus did not refer to the teaching of the rabbis as the authority for what He said. Matthew 7:29 observes that He "taught as one who had authority, and not as their teachers of the law."

One of the most significant differences between Jesus and the rabbis was His willingness to teach the multitudes (Matthew 5:1–2). The rabbis usually taught only a select few. The religious leaders of His day viewed the masses with contempt (John 7:49). Jesus, on the other hand, felt compassion for them "because they were harassed and helpless, like sheep without a shepherd" (Matthew 9:36).

His Welcome to Women

One of His most radical departures from the norm was His willingness to accept women as disciples and openly teach them. Women did not usually study the Torah. New Testament scholar Joachim Jeremias has noted that rabbinical custom reflected an attitude which assumed that women were inferior to men. Women were not allowed to go as far into the temple in Jerusalem as men but were restricted to the court of the Gentiles and the court of women. The section of the local synagogue that was devoted to the teaching of the scribes was open only to men and boys. One rabbi who lived around A.D. 90 was even said to have declared: "If a man gives his daughter a knowledge of the Law, it is as though he taught her lechery."

Jesus, however, praised Mary, the sister of Lazarus, for sitting at His feet and listening to His teaching (Luke 10:39–42). He discussed theology with the woman of Samaria and chose women to be the first ones to see Him following His resurrection (John 4:1–39; Matthew 28:8–10).

DISCIPLESHIP IN THE EPISTLES

The practice of disciple making did not end with Jesus. Although the New Testament does not refer to the "disciples of Peter" or "the disciples of John," Christian tradition says that Jesus' disciples eventually gathered their own disciples and trained them to be the church's next generation of leaders. The New Testament epistles also clearly indicate that the apostle Paul followed Jesus' pattern. He urged others to "follow my example, as I follow the example of Christ" (1 Corinthians 11:1). The term in this verse that is translated "follow my example" literally meant "to mimic." Paul openly admitted that he had not yet attained spiritual perfection, yet he urged others to imitate him (Philippians 3:17). His function as a role model was not limited to matters of doctrine. He urged the Thessalonians to follow his example as an employee (2 Thessalonians 3:7–8). Paul took other disciples like Timothy and Titus under his wing and served as their mentor (1 Corinthians 4:16–17; 2 Corinthians 8:17–18). They traveled with him, listened to his teaching, and were sent out on various ministry assignments as Paul's representatives. Like Paul, they were to be living examples of what it meant to be a disciple of Jesus (1 Timothy 4:12; Titus 2:7).

It should be noted that Paul was not always successful in his efforts. Demas, one of those who accompanied Paul on his missionary journeys, eventually abandoned the faith because he "loved this world" (2 Timothy 4:10). Some in the church at Corinth looked down on Paul because they felt that he was not as impressive as other apostles and teachers they had heard. Paul summarized their complaints in 2 Corinthians 10:10 in these words: "For some say, 'His letters are weighty and forceful, but in person he is unimpressive and his speaking amounts to nothing.'"

IMPLICATIONS FOR TODAY

In view of these examples, how should we practice discipleship today? The New Testament emphasizes general principles for disciple making more than it does specific techniques. The discipleship strategy of the early church involved long-term relationships and responsibility for ministry. It included biblical instruction but was not primarily a classroom experience. Biblical truth was lived out in the ordinary contexts of work and church life.

One important implication of this is that *effective discipleship will take time.* Many of Paul's discipleship relationships lasted for years. We are attracted to neatly packaged programs that can be completed in short order. These can be of some value, but are only a small part of the entire discipling process.

Another implication is that true discipleship will involve more than simply "dumping" biblical or theological content. We should not think that once the biblical text has been read, the questions answered, and the verses memorized, the job is finished. While such an approach has the advantage of being compact and provides a sense of closure, *an effective discipleship strategy will also involve practice in ministry.* Jesus taught His disciples and then sent them out. Once their assigned task was accomplished, He brought them together again to be "debriefed" (Luke 10:1, 17). Both Jesus and Paul spent extended periods of time with those they discipled in a variety of settings.

Obviously, this kind of time commitment will limit the number of people we can disciple. In his book *Growing Leaders by Design,* Harold Longenecker suggested that disciple makers invest themselves in three key people each week. He also urged disciplers not to approach these relationships as experts in spirituality. He emphasized that the keys to success include respect, transparency, and patience.[1]

You do not have to be a pastor, missionary, or someone with a seminary degree to be an effective disciple-maker. Eugene Peterson, professor of spiritual theology at Regent College in Vancouver, British Columbia, tells how businessman Chet Ellingsworth functioned as his first spiritual mentor. Ellingsworth often carried out this ministry from the dark and chilly solitude of a duck blind, hidden in the marshes on the Flathead River.

"I can't remember him ever instructing me or giving me advice," Peterson writes. "There was no hint of condescension or authority. The faith was simply there, spoken and acted out in the midst of whatever else we were doing—shooting, rowing, retrieving, or at other times, working or worshipping or meeting on the street and making small talk."[2]

WHO ARE DISCIPLES?

Are There Levels of Discipleship?

Discipleship begins with a personal commitment to Jesus Christ. But how committed does a disciple have to be in order to be considered a "true" disciple? Is every believer automatically a disciple? Or is discipleship something that comes after salvation?

Pastor and author John MacArthur Jr. argues that the distinction between salvation and discipleship is unbiblical. He asserts, "The call to Calvary must be recognized for what it is: a call to discipleship under the Lordship of Jesus Christ. To respond to that call is to become a believer. Anything less is simply unbelief."[3] He points out that the church's mission is not to call people to salvation and then bring them to the point of discipleship at a later date. The church's task, according to the Great Commission, is to make disciples. MacArthur notes that the terms "believer" and "disciple" are used consistently as synonyms in the book of Acts.[4]

Theologian Charles Ryrie, on the other hand, counters that disciples come in all shapes and sizes. He notes that learning and obeying are the products of faith and not the precondition to belief: "If the examples of disciples in the Gospels may be carried over into today, then we would have to conclude that there will be some disciples who learn a little, some a lot; some who are totally committed, some who are not; some who are secret, some who are visible; some who persevere, some who defect. But all are believers (or at least professing believers who have been baptized)."[5]

How Does the New Testament Use the Term Disciple?

The New Testament uses the term *disciple* in some cases to refer to those who were fully committed to Jesus Christ, in others to those whose commitment was questionable, and in some cases to those who eventually abandoned Him. Matthew recounts two men who followed Jesus with reservation. The first, a teacher of the Mosaic Law, promised to follow Jesus anywhere that He would go. Instead of commending him for this, Jesus warned, "Foxes have holes and birds of the air have nests, but the Son of Man has no place to lay his head" (Matthew 8:20). The other man asked that he be allowed to bury his father before following Jesus. Jesus' reply reveals the level of commitment that He expected from His followers: "Follow me, and let the dead bury their own dead" (v. 22). Both seem to have believed that they could follow Jesus on their own terms. Were they actually disciples? The biblical text says that they were (v. 21). It is possible, however, that the term *disciple* is used here in the more general sense of "follower."

In a few instances the New Testament uses the term *disciple* to refer to those who later abandoned Jesus Christ. John 6, for example, tells how some of Jesus' followers became offended with the strong language He used to emphasize that He alone was the source of eternal life. In particular, they were offended by Jesus' assertion that "unless you eat the flesh of the Son of Man and drink his blood, you have no life in you" (John 6:53). "This is a hard teaching," they complained. "Who can accept it?" (v. 60).

Instead of sympathizing with their concern, Jesus followed this hard saying with another that was equally difficult to accept. First, He clarified that when He had said this, He was not speaking in literal terms. "The Spirit gives life;" He explained, "the flesh counts for nothing. The words I have spoken to you are spirit and they are life" (John 6:63).

Next, Jesus acknowledged that not everyone who followed Him actually believed in Him: "This is why I told you that no one can come to me unless the Father has enabled him" (John 6:65). At this point many of Jesus' disciples stopped following Him (v. 66). New Testament commentator Leon Morris noted that the term *disciples* is used in a broad sense in this passage: "A wider circle than the twelve is meant. The reference is to those who had attached themselves loosely to Jesus, but without giving much consideration to the implications."[6]

Even more striking is the New Testament's use of the term *disciple* to refer to Judas (Matthew 10:4; 11:1; 20:17). Although Judas was numbered among the disciples, it is clear that he was never a true believer. Jesus even referred to him as a "devil" (John 6:70; cf. 6:64).

The Role of Grace and the Presence of Spiritual Fruit

MacArthur acknowledges that not every disciple in the New Testament was a Christian but asserts that every Christian is a disciple.[7] Despite their significant differences, both MacArthur and Ryrie agree on important fundamental points. Both agree, for example, that salvation is by grace alone through faith in Jesus Christ.[8] Both agree that God's grace always produces spiritual fruit in the life of the believer. MacArthur explains that grace is dynamic and transforming: "God's grace is not a static attribute whereby He passively accepts hardened, unrepentant sinners. Grace does not change a person's standing before God yet leave his character untouched."[9] Similarly, Ryrie observes that salvation will inevitably lead to spiritual fruit: "As long as the Spirit lives within, no believer can show nothing of the work of salvation and thus be totally carnal all of his life."[10]

MacArthur cannot identify how much change must take place before a professing believer can be validated as a genuine believer with certainty. Likewise, while Ryrie acknowledges that a true believer can be "carnal," he cannot say how much "carnality" would ultimately prove that a professing believer was not a true believer. There is no objective measure.

What is clear is that there is an important dimension of Spirit empowered human responsibility in the discipleship relationship. Grace and obedience are not at odds with one another in the gospel. Both aspects of the salvation experience are emphasized by the apostle in 2 Timothy 2:19: "Nevertheless, God's solid foundation stands firm, sealed with this inscription: 'The Lord knows those who are his,' and, 'Everyone who confesses the name of the Lord must turn away from wickedness.'"

In one sense, both Ryrie and MacArthur are correct. There is a volitional dimension to Christian discipleship. This does not mean, however, that discipleship is optional. If we know Jesus Christ as Lord and savior, we are already His disciples. All that remains to be decided is the kind of disciples we will be.

MAKING DISCIPLES THE OLD-FASHIONED WAY

To what extent, then, should Jesus' pattern of disciple making control our efforts? Are modern methods acceptable? Or should we go back to making disciples "the old-fashioned way"? If this is primarily a question of specific methodology, the answer must be no. Jesus' pattern should not be viewed as the norm today when making disciples.

After analyzing Jesus' approach to discipleship, Lawrence O. Richards made this surprising observation: "Despite the insights that we may gain from studying the teaching methods utilized by Jesus, and despite the value of some of the processes that may be derived from such a study, the truth is that Jesus' discipling method is not directly applicable to Christian nurture in the church."[11]

In fact, Richards went so far as to assert that Christian leaders are forbidden to apply Jesus' methodology in the body of Christ. This is because His method was based upon the cultural model of first-century Judaism, which produced a class of elite leaders, a practice that Christ Himself forbade His disciples to imitate (Matthew 23:9–12; cf. Matthew 20:25–28). "Jesus explicitly rejects the elitist structure of first century Judaism and of the secular world" Richards explained. "Their hierarchical relationships are to be replaced by an egalitarian family relationship, in which all are brothers, and in which the greatest are those who dedicate themselves to serve."[12]

Furthermore, if we are honest, we must admit that it would be unrealistic for the church to take Jesus' methodology as a model for its disciple making today. Jesus required His disciples to abandon their employment and in some cases even their families and to travel extensively with Him. They ate, lived, and slept with Him for approximately three years.

Some might suggest that today's Bible colleges and seminaries come closest to reproducing this kind of experience. Yet even in these instances, the philosophy and methodology which is employed is primarily drawn from secular models of education. Their programs, although intensive, still fall short of the level of involvement that Jesus required of His disciples in the Gospels. They were trained without campus or classroom. They were itinerant students, traveling from village to village with Christ. If this is the only effective way to make disciples, then we can be fairly sure that the church will produce very few.

If, on the other hand, the question of whether we should take Jesus as our example in disciple making is framed in terms of overall mission and general principle, the answer must be yes. The church has been called to follow Jesus' example and make disciples of all nations. Its primary goal is not to mount programs, fill pews, or construct buildings, although each of these may be a legitimate outgrowth of fulfilling its mission. The church's primary goal is to lead people into a lifestyle of full commitment to Jesus Christ (Matthew 28:19).

Jesus' example provides us with a model in this general respect: It is a relational approach. When it comes to the challenge of making disciples in the twenty-first century, it must still be done the old-fashioned way. Disciple making is not a matter of programs but of people. It still takes a disciple to make a disciple.

THE LEARNER
AS TEACHER

DISCIPLES
MAKING DISCIPLES

In his book *Leap Over a Wall,* Eugene Peterson told of the
time he was having dinner with a few friends and had asked
them to talk about a person whose words or actions had shaped
their lives in a spiritually formative way. When each story had
been told, Peterson noticed a common but surprising similarity
among them.

"When everyone around the table had contributed, I noticed while each story had included details that were formative (and sometimes critical) in our entering or continuing the
Christian life, not one of them had been about a pastor or
professor, missionary or evangelist."[1]

That is not to say that people who served in these roles played
no part in the ongoing spiritual development of Peterson's
friends; undoubtedly they had. But what impressed Peterson
the most was the fact that God had chosen to use ordinary people to help his friends make significant advances in their spiritual life. Based upon this, Peterson drew an important conclusion.

"Evidence mounts: Most of what I experience and have experienced in the way of help, encouragement, and wisdom in the actual day-by-day believing and praying, loving and hoping, helping and persevering, obeying and sacrificing in the name and for the sake of Jesus comes from people who aren't considered competent to give it."[2]

When I first read Peterson's observation, I thought of the conversation I had several years ago with Tom, a new Christian who had just begun attending the church I was pastoring at the time. We were discussing the yard at the parsonage. "It needs a lot of work," I explained, "but I don't really want to do anything that will take much time or money. After all, it's not my house."

Tom's eyes widened when he heard this. "You're a Christian!" he exclaimed. "It's God's property. You should want to leave it better than when you found it!"

At first I was speechless. I had always thought of it as the church's property. Then I was annoyed. Tom was a spiritual babe. What made him qualified to give me advice on how to live the Christian life? Finally, I was convicted.

I had to admit that Tom was right. More than that, I realized that what he had just said applied to everything I did. If I am Christ's representative, it ought to be my aim to leave every place I have been better than the way I first found it. Every task I perform is an act of stewardship and must be done for the glory of God.

Although it had only been a matter of weeks since Tom had made a profession of faith in Christ, he had already grasped a profound spiritual truth, and God had used him to call me to a deeper level of commitment. The learner had become a teacher.

When Peterson says that spiritual help often comes from those who aren't considered competent to give it, however, I do not think that he is endorsing spiritual incompetence. He is simply observing that discipleship is not exclusively or even primarily the province of religious professionals. Ordinary disciples make other disciples. It is a mutual responsibility that crosses the boundaries of vocation, age, and gender.

Laying the Foundation

Training in the Home

Ideally, the foundational lessons of discipleship are first learned in the home. Ephesians 6:4 contains this command: "Fathers, do not exasperate your children; instead, bring them up in the training and instruction of the Lord." This verse emphasizes two important dimensions to the family discipleship process. One is the positive dimension of training, or education. The Greek term that is translated "training" is the same one used in Acts 7:22 to speak of Moses' upbringing in Pharaoh's household. He was "educated" in all the wisdom of the Egyptians. It is used in Acts 22:3 to refer to Paul's training under the noted Rabbi Gamaliel. In Ephesians 6:4, however, it is the responsibility of the father. This command is rooted in Old Testament practice.

The Law of Moses emphasized the parental obligation to train children. In Deuteronomy 6:6–9, God's people are told: "These commandments that I give you today are to be upon your hearts. Impress them on your children. Talk about them when you sit at home and when you walk along the road, when you lie down and when you get up. Tie them as symbols on your hands and bind them on your foreheads. Write them on the doorframes of your houses and on your gates." Biblical scholars are divided in their opinion over the Hebrew term that is translated "impress" in Deuteronomy 6:7. Some believe it literally means to "whet" or "sharpen" something, thus referring to incisive teaching. Other scholars believe that the term comes from a root that means to "repeat." Either way, it is clear that keen and repeated instruction is in view. What is more, it was often informal instruction. It occurred at every hour in the day and in a variety of circumstances.

Correction in the Home

The second dimension of family discipleship mentioned in Ephesians 6:4 is correction. The New Testament term that is translated "instruction" in this verse is a word with overtones of warning. It is education that takes the form of admonishment. Paul used this same term to characterize his ministry in Ephesus (Acts 20:31).

It is also the term used in Titus 3:10, which says that a divisive person is to be warned and then avoided if that warning is ignored. "Warn a divisive person" is not a positive phrase, but its goal is positive. The aim of correction is to redirect those who are being admonished to the right path. This means that discipleship has a negative as well as a positive side. Warning is as important as training.

If the obligation to train children in spiritual things rests primarily with the family, what should we think of the tendency for many churches to rely upon professional staff and church-based programs to accomplish this goal? It is not unusual today to find some large congregations with individual staff members who minister full-time to elementary age, junior high, and high school children. Certainly, children's pastors and youth programs have a place in the church. Israel had its priests who were charged with the responsibility of teaching God's people about the decrees of the Lord (Leviticus 10:11). Their ministry, however, as important as it was, was intended to complement the foundational instruction that took place in the home.

Using Various Methods in the Home

Spiritual training in the home during the Old Testament era involved a variety of teaching methods. For example, one important way parents communicated spiritual truth was through storytelling. Israelite parents who had experienced God's deliverance were told not to forget the things that they had seen and heard and were commanded to teach them to their children and their grandchildren (Deuteronomy 4:9).

Informal discussion that was woven into the fabric of everyday life was another tool in this Old Testament discipleship process. Parents were to talk repeatedly with their children about God's commandments as they went about their daily routine (Deuteronomy 6:7–9; 11:19). This instruction, however, was not one sided. Children often asked questions about the meaning of the stipulations, decrees, and laws that Israel was required to observe (Deuteronomy 6:20).

Public worship was also an important instructional tool. Israelite families gathered to hear the Scriptures read publicly (Deuteronomy 31:11–13; cf. Nehemiah 8:2–3). Singing was even used as a teaching device (Deuteronomy 32:44–47).

The overall picture we get from the Old Testament is not one where spiritual training is relegated to one compartment of family or congregational life. Every day was an opportunity to teach and every situation a classroom.

The Example of Timothy

Paul's ministry partner Timothy is a good example of someone whose first discipleship experience began in the home. Timothy's discipleship experience began at an early age. Since his father was not a believer, Timothy's mother and grandmother shouldered the responsibility of biblical instruction in the home (cf. Acts 16:1). Paul praised them for their "sincere faith" (2 Timothy 1:5). He reminded Timothy of the value of their godly example and training: "But as for you, continue in what you have learned and have become convinced of, because you know those from whom you learned it, and how from infancy you have known the holy Scriptures, which are able to make you wise for salvation through faith in Christ Jesus" (2 Timothy 3:14–15).

WHEN THE FAMILY HOME
EXCLUDES SPIRITUAL TRAINING

God at Work

Timothy had the advantage of being taught the Scriptures "from infancy," but many of us come from homes with parents who were not believers. J. Robert Clinton has observed that in such a case God still works through our family background to prepare us to serve Him: "You might find it hard to believe that God was working through your family or your environment, especially if these were not godly influences, but He was."[3] In the case of those who have unbelieving parents, however, this process is more indirect. God works through the providential ordering of our lives, often teaching us lessons that are difficult to see at the time.

Significant spiritual input may not come until later in life. When it does, God helps us to make sense of valuable lessons learned primarily by experience: "It is exciting to see how the providence of God was—and is—working through all our experiences."[4]

Whether or not you have had the advantage of being taught the Scriptures from infancy, you can be confident that God's perfect timing and His providential ordering of your life have laid a valuable foundation for your spiritual life and ministry.

The psalmist marveled that God was aware of him while he was still in the womb. "My frame was not hidden from you when I was made in the secret place. When I was woven together in the depths of the earth, your eyes saw my unformed body. All the days ordained for me were written in your book before one of them came to be" (Psalm 139:15–16). Commenting on the psalmist's words, Charles Spurgeon noted, "God saw us when we could not be seen and he wrote about us when there was nothing of us to write about."[5]

Our Family and God's Work

Our family background and life experiences, no matter how unlikely, were not accidental. They are all part of God's larger plan. This was how the apostle Paul viewed his own personal history. He did not believe that God's purpose for his life began only when he trusted in Christ. He had been raised in Judaism and was once a persecutor of the church. Yet when the time was right, God, who had set Paul apart from birth, revealed Christ to him and called him to apostolic ministry (Galatians 1:13–16).

The Bible offers no more vivid example of this principle at work than in the Old Testament account of the life of Joseph. Born into a family that many today would describe as "dysfunctional," Joseph was favored by his father and horribly mistreated by his brothers. Jealousy and greed prompted Joseph's brothers to throw him into a deep pit and then sell him into slavery (Genesis 37:1–36).

Once the young brother was in Egypt, those who had purchased Joseph sold him again to an important Egyptian official named Potiphar. At first, Joseph experienced a measure of success while serving in Potiphar's household. But when he rejected the attempts of his master's wife to seduce him, she accused him of attempted rape and had him thrown into prison.

In time he was released from prison and became almost as powerful as Pharaoh. Joseph married, and eventually he was reunited with his family, when they came down to Egypt to buy bread during a famine. Yet many things in Joseph's life were never the same. He may have been the second most powerful man in Egypt, but he remained Pharaoh's servant for the rest of his life. Although his father, brothers, and he reunited, he would never return to his home. Joseph eventually died in Egypt, having returned only once to his native land to bury his father (Genesis 50:14, 22).

From a human perspective, Joseph had every reason to be bitter. In fact, Joseph's brothers were so afraid he would seek revenge that after his father died, they falsely claimed that he had sent a message to Joseph begging him to forgive them. According to Genesis 50:18–20: "His brothers then came and threw themselves down before him. 'We are your slaves,' they said. But Joseph said to them, 'Don't be afraid. Am I in the place of God? You intended to harm me, but God intended it for good to accomplish what is now being done, the saving of many lives.'"

They expected Joseph to "hold a grudge against us and [pay] us back for all the wrongs we did to him" (50:15), but Joseph had learned to see God's hand behind all the things he had suffered in his life. God's providence was at work in all his experiences, both the good and the evil.

DISCIPLESHIP THROUGH MENTORING

Modeling Through Behavior

Paul attested to the value of family-based training when he said that he had no other colleague like Timothy, who cared more for the interests of Christ than for his own (Philippians 2:19–21). But parental instruction was not the only influence in Timothy's life. God also used Paul as a mentor to refine the lessons Timothy had learned at home. Paul became his spiritual father and trained him in ministry (Philippians 2:22; cf. 2 Timothy 1:2). Timothy served a kind of spiritual apprenticeship with Paul. He traveled with Paul on his missionary journeys and often acted as his representative (Acts 16:1–4; 19:22). Paul, in turn, served as Timothy's role model. So much so, in fact, that when Paul wanted the Corinthians to imitate his behavior, he sent Timothy to remind them of his way of life (1 Corinthians 4:16–17).

In his epistles, Paul describes Timothy as a "fellow worker," a "son," a "brother," and a "servant" (Romans 16:21; 1 Corinthians 4:17; 2 Corinthians 1:1; Philippians 1:1). Paul felt a deep affection for Timothy, referring to him as his "true" and "dear" son (1 Timothy 1:2; 2 Timothy 1:2). He prayed for Timothy regularly and was aware of his weaknesses (1 Timothy 4:12; 2 Timothy 1:6–7).

Mentoring was not unique to Paul and Timothy. Paul told older women to be reverent in their behavior so that they could "train the younger women to love their husbands and children, to be self-controlled and pure, to be busy at home, to be kind, and to be subject to their husbands, so that no one will malign the word of God" (Titus 2:3–5). This kind of training involved informal modeling through behavior. It did not take place in a classroom but in the context of daily living. It probably did not involve a scheduled time for teaching or a formal curriculum because its lessons were more "caught" than "taught."

Like the approach to training outlined in Deuteronomy 6:7–9, such training relied upon daily circumstances to provide teaching opportunities for those who were being discipled. It was a "hands on" approach to teaching that was dynamic, flexible, and intensely relational.

Another type of informal discipleship is seen in the relationship between the husband-and-wife team of Aquila and Priscilla and the gifted orator Apollos. Apollos was a disciple of John the Baptist who taught in Ephesus. According to Acts 18:24–25, he was a powerful speaker and had a thorough knowledge of the Old Testament Scriptures. His teaching about Jesus was accurate as far as his current knowledge went, but it was incomplete. When Aquila and Priscilla, both friends and ministry companions of the apostle Paul, heard him teach in the synagogue, they immediately recognized the deficiency in his message. After the service, they invited him to their home and "explained to him the way of God more adequately" (Acts 18:26).

Types of Mentoring Relationships

In their book entitled *Connecting,* Paul Stanley and J. Robert Clinton have noted that there are three major types of mentoring relationships: intensive, occasional, and passive. Intensive relationships involve regular training in the basics of the Christian faith, spiritual guidance through accountability relationships, and motivation and training through coaching. Occasional relationships involve advice through counseling, knowledge through teaching, and guidance through sponsorship. Passive relationships involve someone who serves as an indirect example.

The level of involvement and the intensity of the relationship differ with each level. Intensive mentoring relationships are deeper and more intentional than occasional relationships. A passive relationship may involve someone who doesn't even realize that the other person regards him or her as a mentor.[6]

Stanley and Clinton say that all three types of mentoring relationships are needed. "When seeking a mentor, don't look for an ideal person who can do the whole range of mentoring functions," they warn. "Few of these exist, if any. But if the mentoring needs are specified, someone is usually available who can mentor to that need. We believe that mentors are part of God's development plan for each of His followers. He will provide as you 'ask and seek.'"[7]

Beginning a Mentoring Relationship

Most of us have already been involved in mentoring relationships, although we may not have thought of the relationships as such. When our parents or grandparents served as role models and confidants, they were functioning as mentors. So were the Sunday school teachers and youth leaders who provided us with spiritual counsel down through the years.

But how do we go about formalizing a mentoring relationship? The first step, obviously, is to find a mentor. Begin by taking a careful look at your relationships. Who inspires you to grow closer to God? Is there anyone who seems to excel in areas of ministry that are of interest to you?

Look for an opportunity to spend time with the person in settings that will allow you to observe his or her life and ministry. In some cases this may mean getting involved in the same ministries in which that person is active. Or it may mean inviting the person out for coffee to get to know him or her better.

Once you feel comfortable enough, you may want to ask if the person would be willing to serve as a mentor. Be specific about the expectations you have of the relationship and work out a structure for developing that relationship that is sensitive to the needs and realities of both of you. Should you meet weekly? Monthly? Where should you meet? What do you want to happen when the two of you get together? How much preparation, if any, should there be on your part?

But what should you do if you want to become a mentor? How does one get started in this kind of ministry? In the secular realm, some schools have actually asked people to volunteer to be mentors for students. Civic groups like Big Brothers and Big Sisters are really mentoring programs. Similarly, many of your church's youth and children's programs provide opportunities to mentor.

When it comes to adults, however, becoming a mentor is a little like dating. You have to wait until somebody asks. There are, however, a number of things you can do while you wait. The first is pray. Ask God to bring someone into your life whom you can mentor. Second, begin to reach out to those you would like to mentor. Engage them in conversation at church. Invite them to your home and begin to socialize with them outside the church setting. Mentoring is a relational ministry.

Finally, remember that you don't necessarily have to wear the label of "mentor" in order to be a mentor. Most of the people who I would name as "mentors" in my life would probably not use that term to describe themselves. If asked, they would say that they were my friends.

QUALITIES OF A DISCIPLE MAKER

Bob Johnson taught the Sunday school class I attended as a college student. His friends called him "Bubbles," and it was easy to see why. He had a sense of humor that was so infectious I would often begin laughing uncontrollably before he had finished the first few sentences of a joke. Bob was an electrician with the heart of a pastor. He was an enthusiastic song leader and an interesting speaker.

Being Available

But what I remember most about Bob was his availability. For him, teaching class on Sunday morning was only a small part of his ministry. He often took us with him when he visited student commuters in their homes on Monday nights. He hosted a Bible study for the class on Sunday night after the evening service. If I happened to stop by his house during the week around dinner time, his wife, Ann, would set a place for me at the table and ask me to stay. On one occasion I even showed up unannounced at their cabin in northern Michigan while they were on vacation! Bob and Ann welcomed me as if I were one of their own children and asked me to spend the night. Now, nearly thirty years later, I can see traces of their influence on my life, my marriage, and my ministry.

Effective disciple making begins with availability. It takes time to make disciples. This is implied in the statement of Mark 3:14, which says that Jesus appointed twelve "that they might be with him." He spent extended periods of time with three of his disciples, Peter, James, and John (Matthew 17:1; Mark 5:37; 13:3–4; 14:33). These three were later regarded as "pillars" in the early church (Galatians 2:9).

Evangelist Leighton Ford has noted, "Jesus' leadership development of his undershepherds was not so much a course or a curriculum as it was a shared life. It was an experience of fellowship."[8]

Being Transparent

Disciple making is as much a matter of modeling as it is teaching. Since the disciple maker's life is the content of the curriculum, one of the most important characteristics of a disciple maker is transparency.

This was an important principle in Paul's ministry. His approach to ministry combined "plain speaking" with "plain living." He wrote to the believers at Corinth, "Since, then, we know what it is to fear the Lord, we try to persuade men. What we are is plain to God, and I hope it is also plain to your conscience. We are not trying to commend ourselves to you again, but are giving you an opportunity to take pride in us, so that you can answer those who take pride in what is seen rather than in what is in the heart" (2 Corinthians 5:11–12).

Teaching was an important part of Paul's discipleship ministry. But the example of his life was equally important. In 2 Corinthians 6:4 he gives an impressive list of the kinds of circumstances in which he served as a model for others. These included general affliction, suffering at the hands of others, and hardships caused by self-imposed discipline. In all of this, Paul's goal was not merely to communicate a body of doctrine, although that was certainly part of his aim. Ultimately, his desire was to communicate his heart. "We have spoken freely to you, Corinthians, and opened wide our hearts to you," he wrote. "We are not withholding our affection from you, but you are withholding yours from us. As a fair exchange—I speak as to my children—open wide your hearts also" (2 Corinthians 6:11–13).

Genuine transparency means that others will see our weaknesses as well as our strengths. The biblical model of disciple making is not the Eastern notion of an enlightened guru who has reached a state of perfection but of a fellow struggler who encourages others as they both experience the same growth process. In his book *Mentoring: The Strategy of the Master,* Ron Lee Davis warned that there is little to be learned from a mentor who seems to breeze effortlessly through life: "The value of the mentoring process lies in watching a person of genuine wisdom and character surmount obstacles, solve problems, and overcome mistakes. The secret to profoundly influencing others as a mentor lies in honestly, transparently opening our lives for inspection, warts and all."9

Jesus, of course, is the exception to this. "He committed no sin, and no deceit was found in his mouth" (1 Peter 2:22). He never sinned and cannot provide a model of recovery from failure. He did, however, provide an example of patient learning in the midst of affliction. Hebrews 5:8–9 says that "he learned obedience from what he suffered, and, once made perfect, he became the source of eternal salvation for all who obey him."

One of the first conversations I had with John Natelborg, the campus staff worker for the InterVarsity chapter I attended while in college, had to do with my devotional life. As a young believer who did not grow up in a Christian home, I found it difficult to pray and read my Bible on a regular basis. I had just read a booklet that described Martin Luther's devotional life and was impressed by the fact that his prayer time was measured in hours while mine was measured in minutes. I determined to change and had resolved to spend an hour each morning in prayer and an hour reading the Bible.

John listened patiently to my plan and then smiled and told me how he also struggled with his devotional life. "I admire your goal," he said, smiling. "But it might be more realistic if you began with ten minutes a day and worked your way up from there."

It was probably the best spiritual advice I ever received. John's honesty about his own struggle in this area gave me the courage (and the permission) to set a reasonable goal for my devotional life that served as a foundation for years to come. His interest in my spiritual life did not end when I graduated from college. During the years that followed, we continued to correspond with one another. I wrote to him about my struggles as a young seminary student, a fledgling pastor, and eventually a college professor. His letters have always been marked with the same kind of honest self-reflection that he demonstrated over a cup of coffee in the student union.

THE MINISTRY OF THE FACILITATOR

J. B. Stillson was visiting the ships and lodging houses along the Chicago River in the spring of 1857, passing out gospel tracts and preaching to the seamen he met, when he noticed a stout twenty-year-old doing the same and struck up a conversation with the young man. He found that the young man shared Stillson's passion for telling others about Christ. The twenty-year-old asked Stillson to take him under his wing, admitting that he wanted to serve the Lord but did not really know how to go about it.

Stillson agreed, and the two began to work together inviting children to attend Sunday school, visiting those who were in hospitals and in jails, and evangelizing sailors. Stillson also began to teach his young friend how to study the Bible, who up until then, had been opening it at random and studying any passage that caught his eye. Stillson showed him the importance of studying each passage in context and how to use a Bible dictionary and concordance. He taught him how to pray, making it a point to spend a significant amount of time asking for God's blessing before the two set out for an evening of ministry together.[10]

Today, nearly one hundred fifty years later, few know who J. B. Stillson was. On the other hand, Dwight L. Moody, the young man he discipled, is widely known as the leading American evangelist of the nineteenth century, and the effects of Moody's ministry continue to be felt around the globe.

Disciple making is a ministry of service. It is work that benefits others. The primary goal in disciple making is to help someone else reach his or her full potential in Christ. This was the goal that motivated the apostle Paul to want to visit the believers at Rome. "I long to see you," he wrote, "so that I may impart to you some spiritual gift to make you strong" (Romans 1:11). Paul saw himself as a servant to others in the church (2 Corinthians 4:5). Peter uses the language of stewardship in 1 Peter 4:10: "Each one should use whatever gift he has received to serve others, faithfully administering God's grace in its various forms."

The phrase "faithfully administering" is literally "as good stewards" in the Greek text. A steward was a household manager charged with the responsibility of caring for someone else's possessions. Jesus used the metaphor of stewardship to illustrate the need to be ready for His return. "Who then is the faithful and wise manager, whom the master puts in charge of his servants to give them their food allowance at the proper time? It will be good for that servant whom the master finds doing so when he returns. I tell you the truth, he will put him in charge of all his possessions" (Luke 12:42–44).

Disciple making is an important part of the church's ministry of stewardship. It is the stewardship of people.

In the business world, corporate executives sometimes speak of their "human capital." Successful corporations understand that their most valuable resource does not lie in the buildings or equipment that provide the infrastructure for what they do. As important as these things are, a company's most valuable asset is its people. Perhaps this should be obvious. Beautiful buildings and up-to-date equipment cannot think or plan. They cannot respond to a crisis or develop a new strategy. A business that pays more attention to its buildings than it does to its people is destined to be unsuccessful in the long run.

"It's About People"

In their book entitled *First, Break All the Rules,* Marcus Buckingham and Curt Coffman review the results of a recent survey by the Gallup organization of over a million employees from many different companies. The goal was to discover what a company needs to do to keep its most talented employees. In their book, Buckingham and Coffman point out that today's institutional investors increasingly recognize the importance of people to a company's bottom line. "Traditionally they focused on hard results like return on assets and economic value added." Today, however, they are just as interested in the way a company treats its people. "Today more than ever," they warn, "if a company is bleeding people, it is bleeding value."[11]

If this is true of a business, it is doubly true of the church. The church building is a useful tool, but it is not the church. The New Testament epistles were written to people, not buildings. Church programs are often a good way to deliver the church's ministry, but in the end its ministry must be performed by people. Yet our strategy has often been to base our ministry strategy primarily on buildings and programs rather than on the people who make ministry happen. Making disciples is a matter of investing time, energy, and even finances in the church's human capital.

One of the greatest obstacles we face in making disciples is the church's tendency to allocate its resources based on the amount of return it will receive for the time, effort, and money it has expended. A church that is investing much of its energy and money discipling children or teens, for example, may begin to question the value of such a ministry when it sees that it does not help the church's attendance figures. Or it may want those that it disciples to devote their energy to the church's own programs. Recently I met with a group of leaders from a church that has a large number who work for a nearby parachurch organization. They were frustrated because these members "weren't doing anything" in the church. In reality, their church provided a spiritual base for these members to engage in extended ministry elsewhere.

The church itself may not have reaped an immediate benefit from its discipleship effort, but the body of Christ did. The New Testament church of Antioch must have understood this principle or it would not have sent its most skilled members to make disciples elsewhere (Acts 13:1–3). A discipleship strategy that is based solely on the benefit the church receives in return robs God.

In the end, disciple making is a function of relationships within the church rather than programs or specific methodology. It is Paul becoming a spiritual father to Timothy. It is J. B. Stillson adopting D. L. Moody as his apprentice in evangelism. It is Bob Johnson gladly sharing his vacation with an uninvited guest.

In the final analysis, discipleship is a "people" thing. Through it God uses ordinary people to do the extraordinary work of transforming lives.

t   w   e   l   v   e

THE CORPORATE CONTEXT OF DISCIPLESHIP

THE IMPORTANCE OF THE LOCAL CHURCH

In his autobiography, Augustine told the story of the Roman orator and educator Victorinus. He was a noted philosopher and a tutor to many of the members of the Roman senate. A statue had been erected in his honor in the Roman forum. He was deeply interested in pagan philosophy but had also studied Christian literature.

At one point, Victorinus told Simplicianus, the bishop of Milan, "I want you to understand that I am already a Christian."

Without hesitating, the bishop shot back, "I will not believe it, nor will I rank you among Christians, unless I see you in the Church of Christ."

Victorinus laughed and replied, "Do walls then make Christians?"[1]

Victorinus had grasped an important biblical truth. Walls do not make a Christian. The church is not a building. It is made up of people who have been joined to Christ by faith. But his smug reply suggested that he had missed the real significance of the Bible's teaching on the nature of the church. Buildings are not essential to the Christian life, but the church is. The Christian life is a life in community with other believers.

This is especially important when it comes to discipleship. Discipleship is often regarded as a "private" exercise. It is seen as a matter of one's individual practice of Bible study, prayer, and personal obedience. When our view of discipleship does involve others, the circle of those relationships rarely extends beyond the inclusion of one other "discipler" or "mentor." The biblical context of discipleship, however, is corporate in nature. If discipleship is a "people" thing, it is equally true that it is also a "group" thing.

A GROUP EFFORT AND A COMMON GOAL

The corporate nature of discipleship is emphasized in Ephesians 4:11–13, which says that Christ gave "some to be apostles, some to be prophets, some to be evangelists, and some to be pastors and teachers, to prepare God's people for works of service, so that the body of Christ may be built up until we all reach unity in the faith and in the knowledge of the Son of God and become mature, attaining to the whole measure of the fullness of Christ."

When Paul wrote about spiritual gifts elsewhere, he described them in terms of abilities (Romans 12:6–8; 1 Corinthians 12:1–10; cf. 1 Peter 4:11). In Ephesians 4, however, the emphasis is not on abilities given to individuals but on individuals who edify the church. It is the individuals themselves who are the gifts, and their mission is one of discipleship.

God has gifted and given individuals to the church "so that the body of Christ may be built up" (Ephesians 4:12).

The Greek term translated "built up" can refer either to the act of building or to what is built. In this case, it refers to the act of building. As commentator Peter O'Brien explains, "The verb employed here is used figuratively and means to 'attain or arrive at a particular state,' with the focus on the end point. Significantly, Christian growth or progress does not occur in isolation, for Paul's language here envisages God's people *collectively (we all)* as en route to this vital destination."[2]

The ultimate result of this effort, according to Ephesians 4:13, will be maturity. This is described further as "attaining to the whole measure of the fullness of Christ." Discipleship is the process of edifying the church for the purpose of maturity. It takes a multitude of people to accomplish this goal. It is a collective effort with a collective result. But what does this maturity look like? Paul emphasizes three important dimensions in Ephesians 4:13. They are unity, knowledge, and fullness.

Mature in Unity

The first of these is obviously corporate in nature. Unity is not an issue unless there is more than one person involved. In Ephesians 4:13 the goal is a particular kind of unity. It is unity of the faith. Most of the time when we speak of faith we are referring to individual personal belief. This is still true to some degree in this verse. In this context, however, the focus is on what is believed by the church as a whole. It is the body of doctrine that the apostles have entrusted to the church. This is the "one faith" spoken of in Ephesians 4:5 and what the apostle characterizes elsewhere as "the faith of the gospel"(Philippians 1:27). It is a faith that can be taught and must be defended.

Such faith is fundamental: It forms the basis for all that the church teaches and practices. Its truths have moral implications and are to be taught and held with a clear conscience (Colossians 2:7; 1 Timothy 3:9).

Mature in Knowledge

The second component of the maturity described by Paul in Ephesians 4:13 is knowledge. But this refers to a particular kind of knowledge. It is the knowledge of Christ. The doctrine that comprises the heart of the church's faith has Christ at its center. One implication of this is that true understanding of biblical truth leads to a deeper understanding of the person of Christ.

This knowledge has both a cognitive and an experiential dimension. The cognitive dimension is doctrinal in nature. Those who know Christ know Him as He truly is. They acknowledge Him as God's Son, their Redeemer and Lord.

Doctrinal knowledge, however, is not an end in itself. Its ultimate goal is to transform our character. This is the experiential dimension of knowing Christ. It is knowledge that is put into practice. John stresses the importance of this dimension of knowing Christ when he writes, "We know that we have come to know him if we obey his commands. The man who says, 'I know him,' but does not do what he commands is a liar, and the truth is not in him" (1 John 2:3–4). The more we know Christ in the sense spoken of here, the more we are changed into His image.

The Final Result: Being Fully Like Christ

The end result of this growth process is the third component mentioned by Paul in Ephesians 4:13: "attaining to the whole measure of the fullness of Christ."

The ultimate goal is to be fully like Christ. Once again, this is not an individualistic goal but a corporate one. It is, in the words of John Stott, "maturity in unity which comes from knowing, trusting and growing up into Christ."[3] Christ is the measure of spiritual maturity both individually and corporately.

THE BODY OF CHRIST

The idea of community is not unique to the New Testament. It is an important theme in the Old Testament as well. The Law of Moses often called God's people to gather as a congregation for worship (Exodus 12:16; Numbers 8:9; Deuteronomy 4:10). They were called the "assembly" or "the assembly of the LORD" (Leviticus 4:14; 24:14; Deuteronomy 23:1–3, 8; Joshua 22:16; 1 Chronicles 28:8; Micah 2:5). Christians share this distinction of being God's people (Hebrews

13:24; 1 Peter 2:10). The church is referred to as "the church of the living God" (1 Timothy 3:15).

The Church in Relationship with Christ

The church, however, has been given a unique privilege that Israel did not share—its relationship with Jesus Christ. The church is the assembly of the Lord, but it is also "the body of Christ" (1 Corinthians 12:27; Ephesians 4:12).

When the Scriptures refer to the church this way, they point to two important dimensions of its relationship. The first is its relationship with Jesus Christ. The church has been joined to Christ. Jesus gave a vivid illustration of this in John 15:5 when He said, "I am the vine; you are the branches. If a man remains in me and I in him, he will bear much fruit; apart from me you can do nothing." During His earthly ministry, Christ promised that He would establish the church (Matthew 16:18).

He remains both the church's builder and the foundation upon which the church is built (1 Corinthians 3:11). He is the "head" of the church (Ephesians 1:10; 4:15). Just as in the human body, the head directs the body's members and organizes their activity so that they function together, Christ directs the members of the body of Christ and enables them to function as a whole. According to Ephesians 4:16, "From him the whole body, joined and held together by every supporting ligament, grows and builds itself up in love, as each part does its work."

The Church in Relationship with Its Members

These words, however, also point to a second dimension of the church's relationship—the bond among the various members of the body of Christ. It is a body that "builds itself up."

The Holy Spirit is the unifying agent in both of these dimensions. The same Spirit that has joined the church to Christ has also joined its members to one another: "For we were all baptized by one Spirit into one body—whether Jews or Greeks, slave or free—and we were all given the one Spirit to drink" (1 Corinthians 12:13).

The practical result of this union is that we need other believers to grow spiritually. There is an equally important corollary to this truth. If we need other believers, then other believers need us.

FEELING INFERIOR OR SUPERIOR TO OTHERS

Feeling Inferior

It is possible to overlook both of these truths in our approach to the Christian life. In some cases we may slip into an attitude of inferiority, concluding that we are not very important to the body of Christ. We may feel that our ministry is so insignificant that the church can function without it. The apostle Paul compared this to a foot concluding that it was not a part of the body because it was not the hand, or an ear saying that it was not a part of the body because it was not the eye (1 Corinthians 12:15–16). In reality, every member contributes to the overall well-being of the body. "If the whole body were an eye, where would the sense of hearing be?" Paul asks. "If the whole body were an ear, where would the sense of smell be? But in fact God has arranged the parts in the body, every one of them, just as he wanted them to be. If they were all one part, where would the body be? As it is, there are many parts, but one body" (vv. 17–20).

The human body cannot function on the basis of one organ alone. If an organ ceases to function, great damage and even death is usually the result. The same is true of the church. Every member contributes to the church's spiritual health. Our gifts and abilities may not be as glamorous as those possessed by others, but they are vitally needed. If we separate ourselves from the church, or refuse to exercise our spiritual gifts, the church suffers as a result.

Feeling Superior

Why do some of the church's members develop this kind of "spiritual inferiority complex?" The sad truth is that they have help from other believers who suffer from the opposite problem. These other believers have developed what might be described as a spiritual superiority complex. Their thinking is reflected in 1 Corinthians 12:21: "The eye cannot say to the hand, 'I don't need you!' And the head cannot say to the feet, 'I don't need you!'" In the church of Corinth those with greater gifts had begun to believe that they were indispensable to the church but felt that they did not need those who possessed the less spectacular gifts. Paul warned that this mentality was irrational and spiritually damaging.

The members of the body of Christ are not in competition with one another. The Christian life is not a beauty contest in which those who have spectacular gifts are more pleasing to God than those whose gifts are more mundane. In fact, in 1 Corinthians 12:22 Paul emphasized that those members of the body who seemed to be weaker were actually "indispensable."

The church's weaker or unimpressive members are essential to its health. God has organized the church this way "so that there should be no division in the body, but that its parts should have equal concern for each other" (1 Corinthians 12:25).

One way that Christians can still practice the error that Paul criticized in 1 Corinthians 12:21 is by approaching their spiritual life from the related perspectives of privatism and individualism. By privatism I mean the tendency to relegate religious belief and the spiritual life to the private domain. Privatism does not deny the value of such things but feels that they are best exercised outside the public sphere. Individualism is the perspective that says that the values and experience of the individual are more important than those of the larger group. They are both exemplified in the comment made to me by a man who, when I invited him to attend church, laughed and replied, "What do I need to go to church for? I can read the Bible and pray on my own. If I need to hear a sermon, all I have to do is turn on the television and I can listen to some of the best preachers around."

Although he claimed to be a Christian, he did not feel that he had a need for the church. His spiritual life was a purely private matter, and the test of its health was measured by his own subjective experience. As long as the time he spent reading the Bible in private was meaningful and the sermons he watched on television were stimulating, why did he need the church? Indeed, he was convinced that he was better off without it. His thinking may have been in harmony with modern society's approach to the spiritual life, but it is sadly out of step with the Bible.

"Our call is not defined in terms of independent or self-reliant efforts," notes Darrell Bock, professor of New Testament studies at Dallas Theological Seminary. The life of discipleship is a life of interdependence. "While each of us answers his or her call of God individually," Bock explains, "we live out that call in shared community. God always calls us into relationship, first with himself, and as an outpouring of that, with brothers and sisters in Christ."[4]

A COMMUNITY OF ENCOURAGEMENT

What, then, should our discipleship experience be like? It should have both a personal and a corporate dimension. The author of the book of Hebrews has emphasized both in Hebrews 10:22–25. He has underscored the importance of personal faith by telling his readers to draw near to God with "a sincere heart in full assurance of faith" and to "hold unswervingly to the hope we profess" (Hebrews 10:22–23).

Spurring Each Other
Toward Love and Good Deeds

Hebrews 10:24 emphasizes the corporate dimension of discipleship by urging readers to "consider how" they might spur each other on "toward love and good deeds." The language used here indicates that the author had more in mind than a casual commitment to the idea of congregational life. The verb that is translated "consider" in Hebrews 10:24 meant to "contemplate" or "look closely" at something. But notice what was to be the object of their study. In the Greek text the object of this verb is "one another." The command is to make a careful study of others for the specific purpose of spurring them on to love and action. This is not an adversarial relationship, where we look critically at each other in the hope of finding some flaw to condemn. Rather, it is a study in encouragement.

The goal of this corporate self-analysis is to understand others well enough to know what will motivate them to live the Christian life more successfully.

These things cannot be accomplished if we isolate ourselves from one another. Consequently, the author of Hebrews adds this warning to his exhortation: "Let us not give up meeting together, as some are in the habit of doing, but let us encourage one another—and all the more as you see the Day approaching" (Hebrews 10:25). There is more in view here than simply a command to attend the worship services of the church.

F. F. Bruce has suggested that the problem may not have been that they had stopped meeting with Christians altogether, but that they had become part of a small group that had separated itself from the larger congregation.[5] Commentator Donald Guthrie agrees: "Some had evidently been neglecting to meet with their Christian brethren and this is seen as a serious weakness. It may be that the readers had splintered off from the main group, which meant that their opportunities to provoke to love and good works were severely limited."[6]

If this was the case, it was probably because the larger fellowship included a mixture of converted Jews and Gentiles. Were they motivated by a fear of what their Jewish friends and neighbors would think if they identified themselves with the church? Did they want to create a "purer" fellowship, separate from Gentile believers? Either way, the result was the same. They were avoiding the thing they needed most: the encouragement of the fellowship of other Christians.

How We Can Encourage Others

Encouragement takes many forms. It may be expressed as a kind word and a pat on the shoulder. At other times it takes the form of a sharp kick (figuratively speaking) in the seat of the pants. One of the ways congregational life helps us in our discipleship is by providing a context for accountability. Paul's command in Galatians 6:1 urging those who are spiritually mature to restore any who are caught in a sin implies a mutual concern for the spiritual well-being of others in the church. For some, this concern will be expressed in the form of confrontation and rebuke. The aim, in this case, is to help others see the spiritual danger their attitude or behavior creates for themselves and for the church at large.

Paul prescribed this kind of "encouragement" for the brother who was overtaken by sexual sin in Corinth (1 Corinthians 5:1–5). He argued that by tolerating this man's sin the church was jeopardizing its own spiritual health. In 1 Corinthians 5:6 he warns, "Your boasting is not good. Don't you know that a little yeast works through the whole batch of dough?" Sexual immorality, however, is not the only kind of sin that threatens to permeate the life of the church when it goes unconfronted. Other seemingly less serious sins are equally dangerous. Among them are greed, dishonesty, slander, and divisiveness (1 Corinthians 5:9–11; Titus 3:10).

The greatest challenge in exercising the church's ministry of mutual encouragement is in striking the right balance. Many churches seem to be given to extremes. A church that is afraid of becoming "abusive" accepts everyone, regardless of lifestyle. Another, out of a desire to be separate, regulates the lives of its members with military rigidity and creates the spiritual equivalent to a police state. Neither of these extremes reflects the biblical pattern.

In the New Testament, congregational encouragement is as concerned with restoration and affirmation as it is with confrontation of sin. Paul urged the Corinthian church to reaffirm its love to one of its members after it had confronted him about his sin. "The punishment inflicted on him by the majority is sufficient for him. Now instead, you ought to forgive and comfort him, so that he will not be overwhelmed by excessive sorrow" (2 Corinthians 2:6–7). The term that is translated "comfort" in this passage is the same Greek word that is translated "encourage" in Hebrews 10:25.

It is the church's obligation to be holy that provides the background for this ministry of mutual encouragement and accountability. The church is already holy in position. It members are described as "saints," a "holy priesthood," and a "holy nation" (2 Corinthians 1:1; 8:4; 9:1; Ephesians 1:1; Colossians 1:2; 1 Peter 2:5, 9). This is not a status that we have earned by our own effort, but it is a matter of grace and divine calling (Romans 1:7). At the same time, we have an obligation to live out the reality of this calling in daily practice. We who are holy by calling are to live such good lives that it causes even those who do not know Christ to glorify God (1 Peter 2:11–12). This calling has both negative and positive dimensions. Negatively, it is a call to avoid "every kind of evil" (1 Thessalonians 5:22). Positively, it is a call to be "eager to do what is good" (Titus 2:14).

A REMEDY FOR WORLDLINESS

If holiness is one of the primary obligations of the church, its antithesis is worldliness. The church has long known that worldliness is a threat, but the term itself is vague. It has often been associated with specific practices like smoking, drinking, and going to movies. So what is biblically defined worldliness? Is it a matter of musical style, the type of clothes we wear, or whether or not someone uses make-up? As noted in chapter 5, Paul identified jealousy and quarreling between believers as marks of worldliness (1 Corinthians 3:1–3). The apostle John defines worldliness as "the cravings of sinful man, the lust of his eyes and the boasting of what he has and does" (1 John 2:16).

The "world" is both the realm of Satan and the domain of the flesh. Whenever we act in the flesh or in a way that is contrary to Christ's interests, we are being worldly. Christ has sent us into the world just as His Father sent Him (John 1:9; 3:17; 17:18). He loves the world but He does not love worldliness.

When Christ prayed for His disciples on the night before He was crucified, He made this request: "My prayer is not that you take them out of the world but that you protect them from the evil one. They are not of the world, even as I am not of it" (John 17:15–16). These words provide needed balance in an age when those of us who are in the church seem to work so hard to reassure those who are outside its boundaries that we are just like them. We are not. There is a fundamental divide between us that can be bridged only by Christ. We are with them while we are "in" the world but we are not "of" them. "The church's strength lies in its being radically different from the world," R. B. Kuiper explained. "The world is darkness, the church is light. But light must shine into darkness in order to drive it away."[7]

Notice, however, that Jesus' prayer does not contain a command to the church to become "otherworldly" or a request that God would make it so. This "otherworldliness" is stated as a matter of fact. We are not of the world because Christ is not of it. The world is a state, not a practice. It cannot be helped.

What is less certain is the degree to which the church's behavior will reflect the reality of this state. The church cannot be of the world, but it can behave in a worldly manner (1 Corinthians 3:1–3; Titus 2:11–12). How do we guard against this?

1. Becoming Sanctified

The first remedy for corporate worldliness is revealed in Christ's prayer. It is individual sanctification through the word of truth (John 17:17).

Sanctification, in simplest terms, is the process of being made holy. We are made holy in a positional sense when we trust in Christ and His righteousness is reckoned to us as a gift. But we are also sanctified in a practical sense as God's Spirit transforms our attitudes and actions so that they become like Christ's.

The primary tool that the Spirit uses in this process is the Word of God. This means that sanctification involves allowing the absolute truths of Scripture to determine our conduct. God uses Scripture to further our "training in righteousness" and to equip us for "every good work" (2 Timothy 3:16–17). It gives us the strength to overcome Satan (1 John 2:14). Knowledge of the truths of God's Word provides the guidance that will enable us to handle even the most mundane issues of daily life with genuine holiness (1 Timothy 4:3–5).

The standard the church's members should use when they hold one another accountable should be one based upon principles drawn from the Word of God. Without this, we would be forced to create our own false standards, based upon personal preferences or cultural practice.

Unfortunately, such false standards have often been the basis for the church's teaching on what constitutes worldliness. "Worldliness is a word that has fallen out of use today," Ed Hayes, former dean and president emeritus of Denver Seminary, explains. "Most recently it got trapped in the garb of twentieth-century separatism. And so it also did in the second century among desert fathers, in the fourth century onward in monasticism, in later centuries by the Hutterites and the Amish, and in contemporary movements organized for withdrawal from society. Unfortunately, worldliness is very much alive and well in our churches."[8]

2. Being Separated from the World

The second remedy for worldliness is to separate from it and associate with others who are committed to Christ and are growing in grace. Paul gave the principle in 2 Corinthians 6:14–15: "Do not be yoked together with unbelievers. For what do righteousness and wickedness have in common? Or what fellowship can light have with darkness? What harmony is there between Christ and Belial? What does a believer have in common with an unbeliever?"

This statement, "Do not be yoked together," reflects a command found in the Mosaic Law. In the Old Testament, God's people were told not to plow with an ox and a donkey at the same time (Deuteronomy 22:10). Paul used this command to point to the danger of casting our lot with those whose values and behavior are opposed to God.

The Corinthians violated this principle in several ways. They regularly shared in fellowship meals at the temples of pagan idols without thinking about the damage it might cause to those whose conscience was weak (1 Corinthians 8:10). They also ignored the spiritual implications of such feasts (1 Corinthians 10:20–21). They submitted to false teachers who took advantage of them because they were impressed with their speaking ability and viewed Paul with contempt because he did not fit their preconception of what an apostle should look and sound like (2 Corinthians 10:10; 11:20–21).

The notion of "separation" from others may make us feel uncomfortable because it brings to mind the image of "fighting fundamentalists," who can't seem to get along with anyone. Or it may remind us of the person who is singled out and ridiculed by others because their behavior is distinct from the rest. But being singled out isn't always a negative thing. When the winner of a beauty contest is named, the other contestants often cry off camera, not because she was singled out but because they weren't. Conversely, if a famous person that we admired were to mention our name on television and say that we were his or her personal friend, we wouldn't feel bad. We would probably try to capture the moment on video and show it to our friends.

SEPARATION: A MATTER OF ALLEGIANCE

For the Christian, separation is ultimately a matter of allegiance. It is living in a way that reflects the fact that God has accepted us as His children through faith in Christ. As Paul emphasizes in 2 Corinthians 6:17–18, "'Therefore come out from them and be separate, says the Lord. Touch no unclean thing, and I will receive you. I will be a Father to you, and you will be my sons and daughters,' says the Lord Almighty.'" The first part of this quote is drawn primarily from Isaiah 52:11, which was originally addressed to those who were to be released from captivity in Babylon. It warned them not to bring idolatrous items and sinful practices with them when they returned to the land of promise. The second part of the quote echoes several portions of Scripture where God promises to be a Father to those who trust in Him (2 Samuel 7:14; Isaiah 43:6; cf. Jeremiah 7:23; 11:4; 24:7; 30:22; etc.).

The biblical notion of separation is a positive concept. It is separation from worldliness through commitment to a personal relationship with God. This means that the ultimate remedy for worldliness is love for God. According to 1 John 2:15, love for God and love for the world are mutually exclusive. One cannot love the Father and love the world at the same time.

Dave, a businessman who was saved when he was an adult, once described the importance of the church with these words: "I feel the tug of the world to be so great that the only remedy I know for it is to be with God's people." Walls cannot make anyone a Christian; that is something God alone can do. True disciples, however, know that despite this they cannot afford to neglect the church. Walls do not make a church, but people do. It is not a building but a gathering of believers who have committed themselves to Christ and to each other.

THE HEART OF THE MATTER

In the end, true discipleship isn't just a matter of what we do. At its most fundamental level, it is a function of who we are. If we know Christ, we *are* disciples. We have entered into a transformational relationship that will ultimately change us into His image. It is a relationship that demands a commitment based upon love that takes precedence over every other relationship in our lives. It is a spiritual apprenticeship that requires us to take up the cross and follow Christ's example. It is a relationship that connects us to the other members of the Trinity and provides entrance into a worldwide fellowship of believers.

True discipleship is not easy. If we were to approach it from a purely human perspective and attempt it in our own strength, discipleship would be impossible. The good news is that what is impossible for us is possible with God. The same Christ who invited the Twelve to follow Him is the Christ who has called us His own. He died and rose again to make us holy. And it is He who has named us His disciples.

NOTES

Chapter 1: The Marks of Discipleship

1. Horatius Bonar, *God's Way of Holiness* (Chicago: Moody, 1970), 9.

2. John Calvin, *Institutes of the Christian Religion,* ed. John T. McNeill, trans. Ford Lewis Battles, vol. 2 (Philadelphia: Westminster, 1977), 1303.

3. Leon Morris, *1 Corinthians* (Grand Rapids: Eerdmans, 1958), 174.

4. Calvin, *Institutes,* 1313–14.

5. C. E. B. Cranfield, *The Epistle to the Romans,* vol. 1 (Edinburgh, Scotland: T. & T. Clark, 1975), 304.

6. Leon Morris, *The Gospel According to John* (Grand Rapids: Eerdmans, 1971), 456–57.

7. William Willimon, "Jesus' Peculiar Truth," *Christianity Today,* 4 March 1996, 22.

8. J. C. Ryle, *Practical Religion* (Grand Rapids: Baker, 1977), 72.

9. Morris, *The Gospel According to John,* 670.

10. Francis A. Schaeffer, *The Church at the End of the 20th Century* (Downers Grove, Ill.: InterVarsity, 1970), 137.

11. C. S. Lewis, *Mere Christianity* (New York: Macmillan, 1943), 123.

12. Ibid.

Chapter 2: The Cost of Discipleship

1. F. F. Bruce, *The Hard Sayings of Jesus* (Downers Grove, Ill.: InterVarsity, 1983), 119.

2. C. S. Lewis, *Mere Christianity* (New York: Macmillan, 1952), 172.

3. Ibid., 173.

4. Thomas Shepherd, "Must Jesus Bear the Cross Alone?"

5. Sherwin B. Nuland, *How We Die* (New York: Knopf, 1994), 6.

6. Ibid., 122.

7. John R. W. Stott, *God's New Society* (Downers Grove, Ill.: InterVarsity, 1979), 74.

8. Ed Glasscock, *Matthew* (Chicago: Moody, 1997), 150.

9. I. Howard Marshall, *Commentary on Luke* (Grand Rapids: Eerdmans, 1978), 461–62.

10. D. Martyn Lloyd-Jones, *Studies in the Sermon on the Mount,* vol. 2 (Grand Rapids: Eerdmans, 1971), 76.

11. Cited in *They Walked With God,* James S. Bell Jr., comp. (Chicago: Moody, 1993), March 11 reading.

Chapter 3: The Obligations of Discipleship

1. Dallas Willard, "Looking Like Jesus," *Christianity Today,* 20 August 1990, 29.

2. Ibid.

3. John Flavel, *The Method of Grace* (Grand Rapids: Baker, 1977), 473.

4. Eugene Peterson, *A Long Obedience in the Same Direction* (Downers Grove, Ill.: InterVarsity, 1980), 148.

5. Os Guinness, *Steering Through Chaos* (Colorado Springs: NavPress, 2000), 61.

6. C. S. Lewis, *Mere Christianity* (New York: Macmillon, 1943), 114.

7. Collin Brown, *The New International Dictionary of New Testament Theology,* vol. 2, (Grand Rapids: Zondervan, 1967), 769.

8. J. Barton Payne, *The Theology of the Older Testament* (Grand Rapids: Zondervan, 1962), 434.

Chapter 4: Spiritual Formation and Discipleship

1. Barbara Kantrowitz, "In Search of the Sacred," *Newsweek,* 28 November 1994, 53.

2. "Religion and the Brain," *Newsweek,* 7 May 2001, 54–57.

3. James Boice, *Foundations of the Christian Faith* (Downers Grove, Ill.: InterVarsity, 1986), 153.

4. Louis Berkhof, *Manual of Christian Doctrine* (Grand Rapids: Eerdmans, 1933), 146.

5. John R. W. Stott, *The Message of Galatians* (Downers Grove, Ill.: InterVarsity, 1968), 180.

6. Charles Ryrie, *The Holy Spirit* (Chicago: Moody, 1965), 32.

7. Daniel B. Wallace, "Who's Afraid of the Holy Spirit?" *Christianity Today,* 12 September 1994, 37.

8. Ibid.

9. D. A. Carson, *Showing the Spirit* (Grand Rapids: Baker, 1987), 41.

Chapter 5: Obstacles to Discipleship

1. John Owen, *Indwelling Sin in Believers* (Grand Rapids: Baker, 1979), 14.

2. Donald Guthrie, *Hebrews* (Grand Rapids: Eerdmans, 1983), 137.

3. R. A. Torrey, *The Power of Prayer* (1924; reprint, Grand Rapids: Zondervan, 1960), 18.

4. Ibid.

Chapter 6: The Machinery of Holiness

1. R. Marie Griffith, "The Promised Land of Weight Loss: Law and Gospel in Christian Dieting," *The Christian Century,* 7 May 1997, 451.

2. John Calvin, *Institutes of the Christian Religion,* ed. John T. McNeill, trans. Ford Lewis Battles, vol. 1 (Philadelphia: Westminster, 1977), 184.

3. Augustine, *Of True Religion,* xliv, 82; as cited in *Augustine: Earlier Writings,* ed. and trans. John H. S. Burleigh (Philadelphia: Westminster, 1953), 268.

4. William J. Bouwsma, "The Spirituality of Renaissance Humanism," in *Christian Spirituality: High Middle Ages and Reformation,* ed. Jill Raitt (New York: Crosssroad, 1987), 238.

5. Marc Lienhard, "Luther and the Beginnings of the Reformation," ed. Jill Raitt, *Christian Spirituality,* (New York: Crosssroad, 1987), 291.

6. Calvin, *Institutes of the Christian Religion,* 894.

7. Ibid., 908.

8. Karl Barth, *Church Dogmatics,* vol. 3, 77; cited in Ray S. Anderson, *On Being Human: Essays in Theological Anthropology* (Grand Rapids: Eerdmans, 1982), 210.

9. Louis Berkhof, *Systematic Theology* (Grand Rapids: Eerdmans, 1939), 195.

10. Ray S. Anderson, *On Being Human,* (Grand Rapids: Eerdmans, 1982), 210.

Chapter 7: God's Gym

1. Donald Guthrie, *Hebrews* (Downers Grove, Ill.: InterVarsity, 1983), 258.

2. Herman Ridderbos, *Paul: An Outline of His Theology,* trans. John Richard DeWitt (Grand Rapids: Eerdmans, 1975), 175.

3. William Willimon, "Jesus' Peculiar Truth," *Christianity Today,* 4 March 1996, 22.

4. Ibid.

5. H. C. G. Moule, *Studies in Colossians & Philemon* (Grand Rapids: Kregel, 1977), 68.

6. J. P. Moreland, *Love Your God with All Your Mind* (Colorado Springs: Navpress, 1997), 65.

7. I. Howard Marshall, *Commentary on Luke* (Grand Rapids: Eerdmans, 1978), 565.

8. J. C. Ryle, *Holiness* (Cambridge, England: James Clarke, 1956), 55.

9. Dallas Willard, *The Spirit of the Disciplines* (San Francisco: HarperSanFrancisco, 1988), 6.

10. Ibid., 4–5.

11. John Ortberg, *The Life You've Always Wanted* (Grand Rapids: Zondervan, 1997), 54.

12. Ibid., 52.

13. B. B. Warfield, *Faith and Life* (Carlisle, Pa.: Banner of Truth, 1974), 230.

14. John Calvin, *Institutes of the Christian Religion,* ed. John T. McNeill, trans. Ford Lewis Battles, vol. 2 (Philadelphia: Westminster, 1977), 857.

Chapter 8: Christian Virtues

1. D. Martyn Lloyd-Jones, *Studies in the Sermon on the Mount,* vol. 1 (Grand Rapids: Eerdmans, 1979), 35.

2. F. F. Bruce, *The Epistle to the Galatians* (Grand Rapids: Eerdmans, 1982), 253–54.

3. Thomas Watson, *The Beatitudes* (1660; reprint, Carlisle, Pa.: Banner of Truth, 1971), 113.

Chapter 9: The Spiritual Journey

1. The details of Shackleton's expedition and escape are briefly described in Eric Newby, *A Book of Travellers' Tales* (New York: Viking Penguin, 1985), 546–47.

2. Melissa Burdick Harmon, "Antarctic Quest: Ernest Shackleton's Splendid Failure," *Biography 6,* no. 4 (April 2002): 80. According to the article, the ad appeared in the *London Times* on 29 December 1913.

3. J. C. Ryle, *Holiness* (Cambridge, England: James Clarke, 1956), 44.

Chapter 10: The Biblical Pattern

1. Harold L. Longenecker, *Growing Leaders by Design* (Grand Rapids: Kregel, 1995).

2. Eugene H. Peterson, *Leap Over a Wall* (San Francisco: HarperSanFrancisco, 1997), 22.

3. John F. MacArthur Jr., *The Gospel According to Jesus* (Grand Rapids: Zondervan, 1988), 30.

4. Ibid., 196.

5. Charles Ryrie, *So Great a Salvation* (Chicago: Moody, 1997), 95.

6. Leon Morris, *The Gospel According to John* (Grand Rapids: Eerdmans, 1971), 382.

7. MacArthur, *The Gospel,* 196.

8. Ibid., 31; Ryrie, *So Great a Salvation,* 17.

9. MacArthur, *The Gospel,* 31.

10. Ryrie, *So Great a Salvation,* 30.

11. Lawrence O. Richards, "The Disappearing Disciple: Why Is the Use of 'Disciple' Limited to the Gospels and Acts?" *Evangelical Journal,* 11 March 1992, 5.

12. Ibid., 9.

Chapter 11: The Learner as Teacher

1. Eugene Peterson, *Leap Over a Wall: Earthy Spirituality for Everyday Christians* (San Francisco: HarperSanFrancisco, 1997), 23.

2. Ibid.

3. J. Robert Clinton, *The Making of a Leader* (Colorado Springs: NavPress, 1988), 44.

4. Ibid.

5. Charles Spurgeon, *The Treasury of David*, vol. 3 (McLean, Va.: MacDonald, n. d.), 263.

6. Paul D. Stanley and J. Robert Clinton, *Connecting* (Colorado Springs: NavPress, 1992), 41–42.

7. Ibid., 45.

8. Leighton Ford, *Transforming Leadership* (Downers Grove, Ill.: InterVarsity, 1991), 200.

9. Ron Lee Davis, *Mentoring: The Strategy of the Master* (New York: Nelson, 1991), 93.

10. Lyle W. Dorsett, *A Passion for Souls: The Life of D. L. Moody* (Chicago: Moody, 1997), 63.

11. Marcus Buckingham and Curt Coffman, *First, Break All the Rules: What the World's Greatest Managers Do Differently* (New York: Simon & Schuster, 1999), 23.

Chapter 12: The Corporate Context of Discipleship

1. Augustine, *The Confessions of Saint Augustine,* trans. Edward Pusey (New York: Collier, 1961), 117.

2. Peter O'Brien, *The Letter to the Ephesians* (Grand Rapids: Eerdmans, 1999), 305.

3. John R. W. Stott, *God's New Society* (Downers Grove: InterVarsity, 1979), 169.

4. Darrell L. Bock, "My Un-American Faith," *Christianity Today,* 8 January 1996, 22.

5. F. F. Bruce, *The Epistle to the Hebrews* (Grand Rapids: Eerdmans, 1964), 254–55.

6. Donald Guthrie, *The Letter to the Hebrews* (Downers Grove, Ill.: InterVarsity, 1983), 216.

7. R. B. Kuiper, *The Glorious Body of Christ* (1966; reprint, Carlisle, Pa.: Banner of Truth, 1967), 270.

8. Ed Hayes, *The Church* (Nashville: Word, 1999), 99.

True Discipleship

COMPANION GUIDE
The Art of Following Jesus

What sets Christians apart as
disciples? Discipleship is not primarily
a matter of what we do—it is an
outgrowth of what we are. If this is
true, others should be able to see the
proof of the reality of our commitment
to Christ reflected in the way we live.

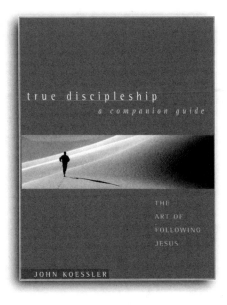

In this *Companion Guide* to John
Koessler's contemplative and practical
book *True Discipleship*, you'll explore

ISBN: 0-8024-1643-8

important themes through the in-depth study of Scripture passages. You'll
find this guide invaluable for your personal Bible study. And you just might
find this study so revolutionary that you'll want to share it with fellow believers
in a group setting as well.

MOODY
PUBLISHERS
THE NAME YOU CAN TRUST.

1-800-678-6928 www.MoodyPublishers.com

TRUE DISCIPLESHIP TEAM

ACQUIRING EDITOR:
Mark Tobey

COPY EDITOR:
Jim Vincent

BACK COVER COPY:
Julie Allyson-Ieron, Joy Media

COVER DESIGN:
Ragont Design

INTERIOR DESIGN:
Ragont Design

PRINTING AND BINDING:
Versa Press International

The typeface for the text of this book is
AGaramond